Albert Ernest Stafford Smythe

Poems Grave and Gay

Albert Ernest Stafford Smythe

Poems Grave and Gay

ISBN/EAN: 9783744718554

Printed in Europe, USA, Canada, Australia, Japan

Cover: Foto ©ninafisch / pixelio.de

More available books at **www.hansebooks.com**

POEMS

GRAVE AND GAY

BY

ALBERT E. S. SMYTHE

TORONTO:
IMRIE & GRAHAM,
26 & 28 COLBORNE ST.

1891.

Entered according to Act of Parliament of Canada, in the year one thousand eight hundred and ninety-one, by ALBERT ERNEST STAFFORD SMYTHE, in the Office of the Minister of Agriculture, Ottawa.

CONTENTS.

FRONTISPIECE   ..   ..
TITLE   ..   ..
TABLE OF CONTENTS   iii
AUTHOR'S NOTE   vi

MISCELLANEOUS.

FLOWERS	9
ROSES	14
SONG OF A WORKER	17
AN OLD CASTLE	20
LOUGH SWILLY	22
NIGHT IN MAY	24
IN JUNE	25
RONDEAU	26
MARION	27
WORDS BY THE WAY	29
BALLADE	30
MAUD	32
JANUARY VIOLETS	35
BIRTHDAY TRIOLETS	36
MARY STUART	37
MY WITCH-WOOD QUEEN	38
LILIES :—	
I. THE CALLA LILY	40
II. THE TIGER LILY	41
III. THE WATER LILY	42
IV. THE LILY OF THE VALLEY	43
WAITING	44
THE OLD WALTZ	46
EVA	48

LOVE LANE	49
LIFE'S FAIRY TALE	51
ASPIRATIONS	52
DARK EYES	54
LOVE'S CONFIDENCE	56
BETROTHAL	57
MARRIAGE MORNING	58
AMY	59
OUR MAY QUEEN	60
DREAM SONG	61
DREAMS	63
COUPLETS	64
KISSES	65
WHO REMEMBERS?	66
SEASONS	68
BREEZE AND BLOSSOM	69
A FORSAKEN NEST	70
GREAT EXPECTATIONS	71
EVANGELINE	72
MY LADY COQUETTE	73
THE CASHIER	75
TRIBUTARY	76
A HAWTHORN BLOSSOM	78
MAY BLOSSOMS	80
ODD AND EVEN	82
THE FIRST WORD	84
BOB AND THE STARS	86
PAUPER AND PUP	88
THE SPECTRE	90
LILIES OF THE NIGHT	92
A CHRISTMAS CAROL	93
A GREETING	94
IN THE TWILIGHT	96

ELEGIACS.

DEDICATORY	98
THE ROSE	99
ONE	101

HER GRAVE	102
EDITH'S GRAVE	103
FADING	104
JESSIE	105
"GOODBYE, MY WIFE"	107
PRIMROSE DAY	109
IN MEMORIAM.—LEOPOLD	111

SONNETS.

THE FORGOTTEN POET	112
NIGHT IN MAY	24
TO A LADY	113
EDITH	114
LOVE BEREAVED	115
DEATH, THE REVEALER	116
AN APPEAL	117
TO HER WHOM IT MAY CONCERN	118
THE LUNAR RAINBOW	119
EVENING LARK SONG	120
AN ACTRESS	121
A PUBLIC READER	122
OF AGE AND LOVE	123
A FACE AND A FANCY	124
IN THE NIGHT WATCH	125
THE SLAUGHTER OF AGAG	126
IN RECOGNITION	127
TO CERTAIN MERCHANTS IN TORONTO	128
A CITY MINSTREL'S MUSIC	129
A BONNET	130

HUMOROUS.

SPARROWS	131
KATE BERRY	133
IN LODGINGS	136
LADY MYRTLE DANCED A WALTZ	138
AN EMPTY PROGRAMME	141
CUPID AND CUPIDITY	143

TRIOLET	146
A CHRISTMAS CARD	147
BABY NEW YEAR	148
A JANUARY THAW	150
VALENTINE	152
FATE, THE MILKMAN	154
EVE WISDOM	155
ONE OF THE LEFT	156
TO BEAUTY ASLEEP AMONG LILIES	158

PEANUT BALLADS.

I. THE PEANUT STAND	159
II. THE PEANUT WEDDING	163
III. A PEANUT LEGEND	168
IV. PEANUT MEMORIES	175
V. A PEANUT ROMANCE	180

AUTHOR'S NOTE.

In the autumn of '82 the writer first discovered himself in the columns of a leading London journal. By permission of the proprietors of the "Graphic" his contribution reappears on page 48. Perhaps nothing that a stern critic might say could evoke chagrin equal to that felt on learning that certain friends and acquaintance had escaped hearing of the occurrence; and perhaps no lenient reviewer could give more pleasure than the congratulation of those who had been more alert. Nine years since then of hardworking commercial life in Belfast, in Chicago, in Edinburgh, and in Toronto might indeed have dulled one's susceptibilities, but as enough spare time has been found for the planning and penning of these pages, so the sensitiveness has not been wholly stifled which derives great satisfaction from a kindly reception.

270 Major Street, Toronto.
    May Day, 1891.

FLOWERS.

The flowers that died in spring-time are the dearest
    we remember,
  They were fair and pure and holy, with the young
    life of the year;
The charm they had was childlike, and the manhood
    of September
  Would forsake its living harvest if the dead ones
    might appear.

But sacrifice avails not when the blessing once has
    vanished,
  The days grow ripe and autumn-houred, the blos-
    soms are no more;
The garden is not Eden, for the Eden hearts are ban-
    ished
  Where vine and fig and olive furnish forth their
    kindly store.

Repining will not bring them, they return no more
    for praying,
  And the dew of tears will draw them not to smile
    upon our ways;
Brown autumn strews the pathway where our mem-
    ories go Maying
  Through the backward-stretching vistas of the
    spring-begotten days.

O flowers that opened joyously, O buds that broke in
    weeping;
  O children of the sunlight, of the kindred of the
    shower,
Still I love to think how human-like you wakened up
    from sleeping
  When the hand of death was lifted, and the winter
    lost its power!

The Apostles gazing wide-eyed from the hillside of
    Ascension
  Had company of angels on the sacred mountain
    slope,
And the flowers are all our angels, in their sweetness
    making mention
  Of the better things to ponder than the failure of a
    hope.

"Why stand ye gazing idly on the firmament above
    you?
  For a season though He left you will the dear Lord
    come again;
Go forward in your faith to those you love and those
    who love you,
  And do service in His vineyard with the sunshine
    and the rain."

So each one tells its message, whether blossoming or
    fading,
  And I dwell on all their meanings till they speak in
    one pure word,

Then the eyesight needs no vision, and the spirit no
    persuading,
  And love reaches to the utmost and the heart of life
    is stirred.

The roots of love strike deeper, and the stems of love
    climb straighter,
  And the leaves of love spread glossier and take the
    breath of day,
The blossom breaks its sheathing and the fruitfulness
    comes later—
  Love's plant of life springs green again and thrusts
    above the clay.

Ah! primrose, pale my primrose, that I folded in the
    pages
  Where I spelled the holy verses in the years of long
    ago,
Your gold will tempt no miser though it fills the
    golden ages
  In the valleys of our youth across the hills, beyond
    the snow.

I plucked you from the cluster long since perished on
    the wayside
  But for sake of simple innocence the thought of
    you endures;
And I wonder, ah! my primrose, will one mourner by
    my clayside
  Give any deed of mine the thought that simple
    worth secures.

Will any wreathe, as I have wreathed the daffodils
    deep golden,
  To cast them on my coffin as I cast them once with
    tears
On his, the gentle-spirited, my friend's, by whom up-
    holden
  The name of old-time chivalry sprang newly to our
    ears.

Unpedigreed and patronless, but kingly-natured,
    clearly,
  All spotless and reproachless, and in speech and
    spirit brave,
His fair name blooms behind him and the airs of
    memory dearly
  Take the fragrance of the noble flowers of knight-
    hood on his grave.

Ah! would it were the only grave where fondest
    flowers are rooted;
  Ah! would it were the only spot where love in
    anguish cries;
How bitter-sweet the token of the claim that death
    disputed,
  This solace of a snowdrop shining where our baby
    lies.

But the flowers return in spring-time, bearing all the
    selfsame sweetness,
  And the spirits that we sorrow for, may they not
    come once more,

With all the old world's wisdom, and with purer-souled
    completeness,
  Till the garden of humanity grows fairer than before!

Then violet, be fragrant still, and harebell, wave not
    vainly;
  We need not fear the winter, and we will not chide
    the frost,
For I hear the voice of Nature, like a mother speak-
    ing plainly,
  Saying "That which I have taken, do my children
    count it lost?"

ROSES.

A BROTHER and sister rosebud
    Grew on a red rose-tree;
The sun in the summer brought them
    Smiles that were frank and free,
And the tears of the morning dew-drops
    Bathed them with purity.

These loving and lovely rosebuds
    Close by a casement hung,
That lighted a room where sadly
    Sickened a maiden young,
And they often across the window,
    Where she could see them, swung.

And she in the weary shadow
    Looked on the happy sky,
And wondered if God thought pity,
    Seeing a rosebud die—
Herself was so very sorry
    Reasoning how and why.

But once, being cheered and stronger—
    Able to rise and stand—
She walked to the open window,
    Stretching her wan, worn hand,
And gathered the latest rosebud
    Ever she saw expand.

That rose was the last gift Nature
    Gave to her dying child—
A fond, but a farewell keepsake,
    Never to be defiled—
The gage of a broken union
    Soon to be reconciled.

She treasured it on her pillow,
    Dewy and fresh and fair,
But it withered beside the fever
    Burning her life out there,
And the rose and the frailer maiden
    Died at the morning prayer.

'Twas the tenderest rose the maiden
    Chose for its greater grace,
And the other with secret pining
    Grieved in its lonely place,
Till its petals that fast unfolded
    Fell to the ground apace.

And while they were faint and falling
    One whom his love had led,
Came weeping to where the maiden
    Lay with her tears all shed:
A rose on her bosom rested,
    Beautiful too—and dead.

There are griefs in the great creation
    Bitter as man has borne,
But the rose's, that pined and perished,

Leaving a leafless thorn,
Is vanity, matched with the sorrow
Many a man must mourn.

Her love was his crown of friendship,
  She was his heart-throned queen,
And hers was the dear example
  Quickened and made him keen
To walk in the path of honour;
  Duty and love between.

"O God, of thy tender mercy,
  Teach me to kneel and pray,
And give me the grace to suffer
  Patiently day by day;
O help me to bear my burden,
  Lighten my darkened way!"

And God in His tender mercy
  Granted the prayer He heard,
And gave him the power of patience,
  Peace, and His holy word:
And he offered his life to Heaven,
  Blest while he ministered.

But ever a rose could waken
  Dreams of the dead old days,
Till he'd think of his Rose in Heaven
  Garnishing God's highways,
And the pain of the early trouble
  Passed into living praise.

SONG OF A WORKER.

The world is very winning
  At the waxing of the moon,
When the harvest is beginning
  And the vintage follows soon.
At dawn the day is smiling
  But I may not watch it then,
Nor when gloaming is beguiling
  Can I rest, nor question when.

With pen and ink and paper,
  With ledger, bill and stock,
With starlight of a taper,
  And moonface of a clock,
I spend my youth and fulness
  In bondage to be free
When half a life of dulness
  Has earned a jubilee.

Who cares my life is friendless?
  Who cares my heart is tired?
Who cares the hopes are endless
  Ambition once has fired?
A thousand hearts are straining
  Against the steep incline;
My brothers, we are gaining
  Gold from a cruel mine.

Yet we who make it duty
   To fight for honest fame,
For truth and art and beauty,
   Love, and a crystal name,
Have tokens on the highway
   And signs against defeat,
And many a forlorn byeway
   Has flowers to make it sweet.

Not hand in hand to conquest,
   But singly and alone,
Knights errant in the long quest
   Each battles for his own;
But achievement brings us nearer
   To the union of the host,
And the victors will be dearer
   Who have overcome the most.

The warriors are graver
   Than the merry sons of mirth,
But their tender eyes with favour
   View the fairness of the earth;
And some summertime hereafter
   They will gather in the shade
Where mellow happy laughter
   Greets fortune long delayed.

But who can join with justice
   In the ease of that far day,
Who toils not where the dust is
   On the hot and rugged way?

Ah! suffering is jealous,
   But perfect love is kind,
And the victory will tell us
   Why destiny seems blind.

What brightens fame in story
   Can make the humble great,
And heads are crowned with glory
   That bowed in low estate;
Then, brothers, unabated
   Be every high desire,
The garlands God has plaited
   Are not for those who tire.

AN OLD CASTLE.

Down the long walk in mouldy solitude
    There stands a castle crumbling to decay,
O'er whose desertion noon and midnight brood
    With melancholy sway.

A dreary mansion, dusty, dim and old,
    Whose doors shut in strange memories of dead cares
Like ghosts that wander sad and unconsoled
    About the rooms and stairs.

A house of contrasts—peacefulness and strife,
    Content and fretfulness, and love and hate,
Sober existence, and light-hearted life,
    The lamb and lion mate;

The idle wanton and the righteous man,
    The faithful servant and the steward unjust,
With all the types that twice a century's span
    Could mould in human dust.

Fondling the moments of a mute caress
    Lovers have lingered in those window-nooks,
And there with hours of labour lost no less
    Men bound their lives in books.

There boon companions led the night astray,
    While close at hand the weary courted rest,
And clamorous curses rose in foul array
    Near murmured words that blessed.

A hundred scenes these haunted limits knew!
   What pleasant parties after festal cheer,
Have said good-night, and climbed the stairs to woo
   Day's death on downy bier!

What generations called the house a home
   Since from the bridal, first its founder came,
Till the last son of sorrow chose his doom
   Of suicidal shame!

When down the stairs the servants slowly bore
   The dreadful burden from the upper room,
Whose shadow clouds and shrouds and evermore
   Surrounds the house with gloom!

No life now dwells where children once grew strong
   And old folk yielded age's slow demands,
Since even Death was there Time has toiled long
   With his relentless hands.

No human sound is ever heard within;
   A phantom race remain its only heirs
Who haunt the rooms and make a ghostly din
   That echoes on the stairs.

Dear heart! shall all our homes thus lie so waste,
   And with the record of our period's peers
Oblivion take ourselves as men misplaced
   Among the newer years?

LOUGH SWILLY.

I CAME through the still meadows
    To where the dead have rest.
Across the Lake of Shadows
    The ranges of the West
    Gloomed to their utmost crest.

A sturdy-pinioned legion
    Bore heavy through the night,
The mountain-guarded region
    Throbbed with the burdened flight;
    The long sea held the sight.

Voices, as from a distance,
    Were swept along the strand
With pitiful persistence
    Crying "we have no hand
    To build the broken land."

"We, warriors of the waters,
    We, lords of towns and towers,
We, chieftains' heirs and daughters,
    We, peers of ancient powers,—
    Earth is no longer ours.

"The days have faded from us
    Fulfilling all their fee,
The sun gives no more promise,
    The night no new decree;
    The shore is as the sea.

"The mountains stand up grimly
    Where the rough tempests beat,
The waters wait there dimly
    Around their patient feet;
    We have no tryst to meet."

Oh, melancholy voices,
    Your passion is not vain;
Unwisely he rejoices
    Who struggles not to gain
    All seasons that remain.

And by the Lake of Shadows,
    Above its clouded face,
I came through the still meadows
    And pondered on Love's grace
    That leaves me yet a space.

NIGHT IN MAY.

BEYOND the hills the daylight dimly sheds
   Some drowsy glances on the restful night;
Thus dreamily the day the darkness weds
   And day is darkened, dark receiving sight.
The cuckoo calling in a far-off field
   Echoes itself to please another spring,
The cry recalling how the past could yield
   Sweet notes and vanish on a swift-flown wing
I love this calmness of the midnight May,
   I love the music of the cuckoo's throat,
I love the beauty of that stilly way—
   The heavens above—where stars effulgent float:
But in this lovely hour I am alone
When I could wish my thoughts another's own.

IN JUNE.

OH! wearily and wearily the days
   Have worn themselves from **winter into June**,
For tardily and tediously delays
   The summer's perfect loveliness of noon.
The sun that soars in heat and sinks in haze,
   The flowers that **wrap** themselves **in scent and
      swoon**,
The wind that hardly goes and hardly stays,
   The lazy birds that chirp a slothful tune,
The quiet rippling **water** running **by,**
   The leaves that rustle loosely **overhead**,
All peacefully I ponder as I lie
   Long thinking in my shady grass-grown bed,
And musing on them for a pastime try
   To realize the winter world instead,
And this seems like a dream before **we die,**
   And that is like a dream of lying dead.

RONDEAU.

Demurely mute as Marion sits
And dreams, or reads, or draws, or knits,
  One might suppose her merely fair,
  But one who knows esteems her share
Of wisdom, and her wealth of wits.

For Marion wears the mood that fits,
And when the merry moment flits
  Returns to some still sweeter air
    Demurely mute.

If that might be which love permits—
A new dream comes, an old dream quits—
  One might forget a buried care
  And Marion hear the new love swear
The old dead vows—love's favourites—
    Demurely mute.

MARION.

I saw the May-moon, Marion,
    Clear charged upon the sky,
Last night in the blue-gray heaven
    Where the day had all gone by.
The same white curve of silver
    I have known for years and years,
No brighter for the smiling,
    No dimmer for the tears.

I watched it sinking, Marion,
    Where late the sun went down,
And the stars came shining lonesomely
    To brood above the town.
And on and on I wandered,
    And through the glaring streets,
And over leafy avenues
    And where the lake-wave beats.

Still thinking, thinking, Marion,
    Of May-moons long ago,
That shone on Ulster hillsides
    And valley-paths below.
Along sweet hawthorn hedges,
    By shadowy field and lane,
Where I heard the corncrakes calling
    And the curlew cry for rain.

I do not murmur, Marion,
   These lonely nights and days,
There is but one companion
   For all the wide world's ways.
You could not know I coveted
   To call you by your name,
Your beauty called me craven
   And put my love to shame.

And you did not stoop, sweet Marion,
   With favour in your eyes,
But evermore your courtesy
   Was kindly, worldly wise.
Ah! how could I approach thee
   With no good gift to give,
But a law of self-denial
   Appointed me to live?

Four thousand miles, fair Marion,
   Make not the distance more;
The distance could not greater be
   That sundered us before.
Not that I yield in honour
   To the worthiest that be,
But the best of all, Mavourneen,
   Were undeserving thee.

WORDS BY THE WAY.

My love, I have no great
    Wise song to sing you;
No vow to consecrate,
    Nor pledge to bring you;
No honour high and rare
    That might renown you;
No fortune fine and fair;
    No crown to crown you.

Only, Mavourneen, a pilgrim forever,
Roaming the world, winning happiness never,
Still would I keep thee—ah! smile if thou hearest,
Deep in my heart with a love-bond the dearest.

    Had you been desolate
        And unbefriended,
    Our ways might wayward Fate
        And Love have blended.
    But Life has drawn you, sweet,
        By paths undarkened;
    I pass your happy feet
        With words unhearkened.

Only, Mavourneen, a pilgrim forever,
Roaming the world, winning happiness never,
Still would I keep thee—ah! smile if thou hearest,
Deep in my heart with a love-bond the dearest.

BALLADE

WITH A BOX OF DAFFODILS.

Of all the flowers that creep or cling
   Or rear a spike, or spread a cyme,
Scattered afield, or blossoming
   Lake-lily-like from mud and slime;
   That suck their life from builded lime
Or wreathe upon the verdured hills
   Young April's artless anadyme
None are more sweet than daffodils.

No garden ever pleased a king
   From Lilliput to Jotunheim
That did not bear the flowers I bring;
   As asphodels of halcyon clime
   Fresh gathered from the meads sublime
Take them, and if your fancy wills
   Their sweetness passes Eden's prime—
You are more sweet than daffodils.

I would that I my heart might fling
   In love's poetic pantomime
Before you as a paltry thing,
   Yet, like these flowers, unsmirched with grime,
   But gallant with a golden rime—
The dust of love—each thought that thrills
   To passion—ah! forgive the crime
You sweeter than all daffodils.

ENVOI.

Marion, when flattery's loud-voiced chime
    Too soon life's early music kills,
Think who, long ere the summer-time,
    Knew thee more sweet than daffodils.

MAUD.

On the Firth of Forth in summer, with the weather warm and clear,
Strangers down at Portobello, strolling idly on the pier,
Should ignore each other totally in theory, but in fact
One's fancies grow to substance and subdue one like an act;
And though person, place, and period may be trivial, we confess
There are tragedies in trifles, and romance in even less.

Maud, I thought you very pretty as you watched a passing crew—
Sailor-costume, hat and jersey, and a frock of navy blue—
Far more fair than all the others, with a look that made you seem
Truer than their little world is; like a spirit in a dream.

When I read your name in silver on the trinket on your breast,
I resolved to do it honour—unknown honour in the West.
And though strangers, life-long strangers—better that than love's decay—
My vow will be unbroken as the silence of that day.
Yet I ponder and I wonder while my vow asserts its claim

How 'twere best to do you pleasure while I linked
 your name with fame,
Such slight fame as I could find you, though we may
 not chance to meet,
But a symbol of the homage I would pay you at your
 feet.

Would you care to be the model for a picture I might
 paint,
Of an aureoled and sombre-clad and grave-eyed maid-
 en saint;
Or the beauty of a ball-room with the dignity and
 grace,
And the splendid stately manner shallow courtiers
 cannot face?
Or you might inspire the music of a melody as rare
As ever floated tunefully around a siren's lair;
Or would you be the subject of a lyric that would
 bring
Its maker greater monarchy than ever crowned a
 king?

Or will you be a memory that comprehends them all,
And lingers loved and lovely all the years that may
 befall;
The vision of a picture to be painted on the heart
And prized above the treasures of a garner-house of
 art;
A strain of softened harmony to tremble on the ear
When day is very distant, and the night is very near;

The echo of an anthem to be heard, but never sung;
The murmur of a poem never uttered by a tongue;
A thread of golden consciousness that once you were
    at hand,
Far gleaming with the hope that side by side again
    we'll stand;
An influence for better on the thoughts that come
    and go,
To raise the lofty higher and to elevate the low;
A watchword prompting nobly till the flag of life be
    furled;
An ever-present witness of the beauty of the world.

JANUARY VIOLETS.

Sing January violets—
   Who ever saw them grow?
Yet my lady has a garden
   Where the north winds never blow.
And my lady moves about it,
   Like a sunbeam through the flowers,
And the year makes haste to woo her
   With the heat of August hours.

Sing January violets—
   They reached me in the snow;
She sent them from a far love land
   Where pleasant waters flow.
Where 'mid the Kerry mountains
   God made Killarney green,
And laid the living glory
   Of Ireland's fairest scene.

Sing January violets—
   It sets my heart aglow
To think what fingers gathered them
   A little while ago.
Before my lady's favour
   The winter frowns in vain,
And summer will be saddened
   Unless she smiles again.

BIRTHDAY TRIOLETS.

OCTOBER is a pleasant time
   Though violets are far away.
Around the fire at even chime
October is a pleasant time,
And falling blythely in its prime
   Your birthday makes the season gay.
October is a pleasant time
   Though violets are far away.

Love's messages ring through the year
   And birthday voices give them speech.
With happy music, sweet and clear
Love's messages ring through the year.
With friendly greeting, kindly cheer,
   And all the meanings love may teach,
Love's messages ring through the year
   And birthday voices give them speech

You know what daring words may dwell
   Among the things a year may say.
When all your kindred wish you well
You know what daring words may dwell
In some one's heart as in a cell
   Imprisoned till a festal day.
You know what daring words may dwell
   Among the things a year may say.

MARY STUART.

Ah! Mary, Mary, queen of hearts,
    Unhumbled by the years,
Thy memory has magic arts
    To move the springs of tears;
The springs of tears and love to move,
    For both fulfilled thy fate;
And still will one the other prove
    And love be weeping late.

Late, ah! so late for me to come
    A mourner at thy grave,
When death has bidden all be dumb
    That would, but could not save;
Late, ah! so late for me to weep,
    Who only know thy name,
When those who magnified thee sleep
    With those who mocked thy fame.

The mournfullest in majesty,
    The queenliest to mourn,
Most beautiful in misery,
    In misery forlorn.
'Tis all the world remembers now,
    But never now to frown—
The glory of a perfect brow,
    The shadow of a crown.

MY WITCH-WOOD QUEEN.

Lonely and lovely, grave and good,
With the innocent-hearted hardihood
Of a maid that walks in a pensive mood
My Queen comes up through the weird witch-wood.

Her presence enlightens the leafy gloom
Of the forest aisles where the shadows loom,
Where the fairest sight is a wildflower's bloom,
Or the lustrous flash of a peacock plume.

Over her, spreading, the green boughs meet,
Under her tread lies a fairy street,
Round her butterflies flaunt and fleet,
Flowers are blowing and herbs grow sweet.

She passes near, but the joy that's bred
In my heart as she comes is a word unsaid,
And all the pleadings mine eyes have pled
Are sealed on my lips with a lover's dread.

I fear to be graceless and overbold
To my Queen meek-hearted,—my Queen high-souled;
And why need she know what my thoughts may hold,
If I love her and crown her with living gold?

Her hair with a sorcerer's wealth endowed,
Has the golden gleam of an evening cloud;
And her glorious eyes that are royal-browed,
Are sunny as morning and pure and proud.

Her brow is peaceful and chaste and fair;
One waits on her words as half-aware
They playfully sweeten or soften like prayer,
And these are beauties a queen may wear.

She comes at morn and she comes at e'en,
And the day is a vision that falls between;
Its sun may shine or its wind blow keen
But the hours lie desert that miss my Queen.

Yet no one knows her, and no one knows
How well I have loved her, for none suppose
I was ever enamoured of more than a rose;
And nobody sees where a man's heart goes.

LILIES

I. THE CALLA LILY.

WHEN the lofty peerless lily,
Silver-browed and chastely chilly,
Hides the dream on which she museth
What a world the poet loseth!
She is queenly on her stem,
Though she wear no diadem,
And she knows she is a queen,
Self-contained, self-ruled, serene;
No supremacy requiring,
No predominance desiring,
Owning such estate of beauty
Reverence becomes a duty.
Thus there dwells the stainless form
Even fancy fails to warm
With the dainty blossom-hues
Morning freshens with her dews.

LILIES.

II. THE TIGER LILY.

Edith's throat of marble whiteness
Shamed the tiger lilies' brightness
Where they blazoned, fiery, flaming,
Their imperial rank proclaiming.
They were proud and passionate,
She was haughty, but sedate;
Heedless in her tranquil pride
Though neglected or belied;
But they courted admiration
And grew faint with emulation.
Thus for contrast Edith wore them
And a comely one she bore them.
They, all eager to be seen,
Curled their leaves with conscious mien;
Edith passed along, too proud
To regard the gazing crowd.

LILIES.

III. THE WATER LILY.

Lonely, beautiful, and stilly
Floats each leafy water lily,
Never rival claim contesting,
Only radiant—only resting
Through a pleasant summer dream
On a gentle, gentle stream:
Dying on the brimming flood
Calmly as they came to bud.
All the lilies, liquid-lustred
With the dew-drops that have clustered
In their shallow, limpid hollows
Where the gnats avoid the swallows,
In the loving waters grow
While their shadows shine below,
But their sheltered hearts of gold
Unreflectedly unfold.

LILIES.

IV. THE LILY OF THE VALLEY.

TINY tinkling bells of beauty
Peal forth elfin calls to duty,
And the fairy people rally
Round the lilies of the valley.
Lady Alice one day took
From the valley where they shook
Such a burden of the bells
Silence fell among the dells.
On her bosom, though, she hung them,
Where her laughter lightly swung them
Till the fairy forces hearing
How they chimed, all came careering,
And they crowded close and pressed
Round her lily-laden breast;
There she bound them—snared with art—
Slaves forever in her heart!

WAITING.

Who knows my own true lover dwells
    Beyond the summer dawn,
Where all the thrilling, chilling spells
    That make the winter wan
Are powerless in the light that throws
A riper ruby o'er the rose?

Who knows my own true lover bides
    In that bright summer land
Where silent time and silver tides
    Creep over soul and sand,
For ever soothing, smoothing each,
The bosom gently and the beach?

Who knows my own true lover lives
    In such a sunny scene
That eager spring-time hardly gives
    The autumn space to glean,
And careless in the close pursuit
The sower tramples on the fruit?

Who knows my own true lover strays
    On shores of happiness,
Where nature decks the dullest days

In some enchanting dress,
And puts her fairest fashion on
To tempt the swallow and the swan?

Who knows my own true lover waits
   To welcome me to bliss;
There, all achieved that separates
   To share it with a kiss;
Who knows how soon the darling hour
Will measure out the marriage dower?

Who knows save only I and he—
   No mortal else beside?
And when men ask how this may be
   A riddle is replied;
Three signs are set to seal this thing—
A flower, a song, a bird's white wing!

THE OLD WALTZ

ALONE in the parlour, alone in the gloom,
With only the moonlight to look in the room,
I waken a waltz from the old yellow keys
Of an old mellow Broadwood of old melodies:
I linger and finger the music an hour
   For the sake of the someone who liked it of old,
And the music is strong with a pitiful power,
   And sombre with secrets that used to be told.
The secrets are mute, though the music remains
All trembling and stirring with dreamy refrains.

Alone in the parlour, alone for so long
That love nearly tires of the sorrowful song;
And nothing has changed but the wearisome years,
And nothing is sure but the shedding of tears.
And nothing has happened for time out of mind,
   And nobody vexes, for nobody knows,
And hearts that were bruised are consoled and re-
     signed,
   Though one heart dreams ever on all the old woes:
The woes that were joys ere the tale was complete,
And the music is saddened that sounded so sweet.

Alone in the parlour, for ever alone,
And the love-music dies in a low minor tone.
I cover my face in a passion of grief
But only the tears ever come for relief.
For the words that would solace forever are stilled,
   The lips that would comfort have breathed their
      last sigh,
The wish that would cheer me can never be willed,
   And all I remember is bidding good-bye.
And all that I learn is the lesson that lies
In the tones of a waltz, and the grief that replies.

EVA.

HIGH, high, in the westerly sky
    Lingers the day as I linger by thee;
Slow, slow, from the darkness below
    Creeps the night over the brim of the sea.

Soft, soft, to the sea-birds aloft,
    Whisper the waters that toss on the shore,
Rare, rare, from the mermaidens' hair,
    Scattered and sparkling, the jewels they wore.

Far, far, there is shining a star
    Pure as the beacon a seraph would burn,
Clear, clear,. that poor wanderers here,
    Seeing it lead them, a pathway might learn.

Soon, soon, will the silvery moon
    Glow through a glory of luminous mist,
Pale, pale, in her vaporous veil,
    Down on the flowers that look up to be kissed.

Then, then, when the children of men
    Seal up their souls with a slumbering spell,
Sweet, sweet—and till morn when we meet
    Angels will guard thee and comfort thee well.

LOVE LANE.

"O WILL you wear a nosegay
    If I should pluck the flowers,
And will it be the dearer
    In four-and-twenty hours?"
"Yes, I will wear your nosegay
    A day upon my breast,
And then among my treasures
    A life-time it will rest."
        They have an old enchantment
           Of scents that never wane,
        And posies are the sweetest
           From Love Lane.

"O will you sing a song, love,
    With magic words of mine,
Of prayer, and praise, and pleasure,
    The olive and the vine?"
"Yes, I will sing your song, love,
    And never may they cease,
The prayer, the praise, and pleasure,
    The plenty and the peace."
        It has an old enchantment
           The song with that refrain,
        But still it sounds the clearer
           Down Love Lane.

"O will you walk with me, love,
　　Low carolling my song,
　And wear my nosegay emblem,
　　And dare to love me long?"
"Yes, I will walk with you, love,
　　Forever and a day,
　The flowers will help to brighten,
　　The song will cheer the way."
　　　　And 'tis the old enchantment,
　　　　　The story told again,
　　　　For all the world must wander
　　　　　Through Love Lane.

LIFE'S FAIRY TALE.

Our lives are like our fairy tales
   With wicked plots and heroes real,
Yet farther fetched the image fails,
   Our loves and beauties are ideal.

But false or true we still love on,
   The dearer often when the vainer;
And he that loves when hope is gone
   I do esteem to be the gainer.

Our purest love is spent in vain,
   Unselfish, suffering, true for ever;
Its bitter unrewarded pain
   Is cleansing fire for all endeavour.

It tries all virtues—to be kind,
   The cares one can to spare one's neighbour,
To prove it is the happiest mind
   That makes the common good its labour;

And life's attainments so refined
   Are finished like the fairy morals,
And all our heroes are assigned,
   "For ever after," happy laurels.

ASPIRATIONS.

I know no love but her my dreams behold
And she is fairest by a hundred fold,
And we shall meet before the years are told.

They say she will not come—she is too rare—
That fate will not embody one so fair
To be a mortal, for a mortal's prayer.

One answers, whatsoever ye require
In praying, think ye have what ye desire,
And 'twill be granted as thy prayers conspire.

But if she came not, could I cease to dream?
'Tis better with its love and faith supreme,
Its dignity, than life of lower scheme.

My daily thoughts do not more aptly taint
Beneath the guiding influence of a saint
Whose character my best perceptions paint.

My work is none the worse that one stands by
Inscrutably, to prompt the erring eye
And wandering hand to fruitful industry.

The pen as freely marks the meaning line,
The digits still as rapidly combine
As when my dearest thought was less divine.

My dearest thought!—that daily grows more dear
That daily challenges a higher peer,
And daily seeks a more exalted sphere.

Whose service still must win my steps along,
Abashed at last the loftiest bards among
Where weakest music is a seraph-song.

Ah! love, while thus in dreams I seek delight
Thyself mayst walk at hand and through the night
To make the morning lovely in my sight.

Even as I stretch my hand and lisp some word,
The dark may lighten, and my dreams be stirred,
True life, true love, begin; my prayers be heard.

DARK EYES.

O DEAR dark eyes! fresh wells of welcome truth,
    Set in a desert world of fraud,
If I might gaze till thirstless, then, in sooth,
    I'd ever look and laud.

How oft the coaxing glitter of grey eyes
    And blue and hazel lured me on
To trouble me, too simple to surmise
    That but a mirage shone.

What bitter pledges have I often quaffed
    From pure-appearing wells of wile,
Blaming myself for sourness in the draught
    Believing eyes that smile

And always smile were always good and true,
    Until I knew the sometimes sad
Grave eyes are truest, best, and rarest too.
    When guileful hearts look glad

Through fascinating eyes, who is deceived
    Finds hid beneath the charming cheat
Sourness more sour, since cunningly bereaved
    Of some expected sweet.

But those dark eyes of thine will ne'er delude:
  They say what is, or well or ill;
Their pleasure swells communicated good,
  Their graveness, with a thrill

Of sympathy, imparts a fated care
  So kindly, half the pain is spared,
For in their depths one sees one does not bear
  The bitterness unshared.

O love of mine! if earth should lose her light,
  And hope be quenched, and sin seem wise,
Then would I look, while all around was night,
  On heaven, through thy dark eyes.

LOVE'S CONFIDENCE.

What fault could be so heinous,
    What word give Love annoyance,
That wrath should over-reign us
    And wrest away Love's joyance?

Though fortune over-shine us,
    Though fate forego her promise,
What chance can unentwine us,
    Or take Love's bounty from us?

We shall be wise, and careful
    To turn from Folly's boothful;
Our love will make us prayerful,
    And prayer will make us truthful.

For truth is Love's ambition,
    And you and I have weighed it;
And prayer is Love's petition
    And you and I have made it.

BETROTHAL.

THE words of love are spoken,
The silver silence broken,
The troth-plight made, Love wears the golden token.

Fulfilment cometh later—
True love's a patient waiter;
Life,—death—are true, and self the only traitor.

There is no fear in waiting
Of peace and joy abating;
Love knows; a prophet—Love—premeditating

When faith can follow fable,
Can suffer and be stable,
Love—knowing truth—is Love unfit, unable?

Go, mark the stars in heaven,
One over-ruling seven,
Far-shining see them, dim, dull, dark, death-riven.

With ever-varying glory
They lighten earth's long story,
But Love will see them change and Time grow hoary.

God's children's hearts are deeper
Than dreams that vex a sleeper,
These human things are treasures to their Keeper.

MARRIAGE MORNING.

ONE sunniest morn among youth's sunny days
   When all the light of life—like that which passed
   The eastern panes, and tinted glories cast—
Was summerhued for me with rainbow rays.

One happiest hour in all the hours I've knelt
   And prayed for happiness. All sorrow-pain
   That ever saddened me returned in vain:
Life's burden fell when love unloosed the belt.

The holiest time in church I ever spent;
   Not there to rest awhile and idly think
   Or dream, but every word with thought to link,
For love was crowned in that new sacrament.

The brightest, happiest, holiest time of life,
   God-graced, and gifted with the smiles of earth;
   A sweet occasion for the spousal birth
Of boy and maiden into man and wife!

AMY.

I was a little lonely maid
And shyly timid, much afraid,
All my world was bare, but the castled air
    Long years ago.

At last there came the handsome youth,
My fairy prince in fancied truth,
But his plighted troth made a broken oath
    Long years ago.

I could not think he would deceive,
And greatly, gravely did I grieve,
Yet forgave the lies of his false bright eyes
    Long years ago.

Another lover claimed my hand,
And bound me with the golden band,
By my wedding ring he's my fairy king
    Since years ago.

OUR MAY QUEEN.

Our May Queen is one for the children—
    She leads them nor needs to compel;
"She is kind," they say, "is our sister;"
    Ah! that is a sovereign spell.

Our May Queen is one for the lovers
    They are faithful and never rebel;
They look, they are subjects, they whisper
    "Her charm is a beauty spell!"

Our May Queen is one for the elders—
    They smile and they say—"It is well;
We reigned or we worshipped like this once
    When Time's was a powerless spell."

Our May Queen is queen over many,
    The reason is easy to tell;
One learns with a little service
    She rules with a loving spell.

DREAM SONG.

My spirit on wings that were strong
    Peeped at Luella's pane,
While the light of the host of the stars
    Fell in a golden rain.
My soul, with the scintillant stars
    Peered in the dusky room,
At the dreams, in a fanciful throng
    Filling the failing gloom.
My soul, like a fluttering dove,
    Beat at the dew-dim pane;
Ah, my spirit was suffering love
    Wooing in vain, in vain,
Benightedly there by her nest
    Cooing a tender strain,
While its mate in her maidenly rest
    Slumbered and dreamed again.

My soul as a butterfly may
    Floated with tiny grace
Through the zephyrous breath of her sighs
    Over her fair fresh face,
And timidly passing her eyes,
    Resting on brow, on lips,
On her bosom it trembled and lay
    Light as her finger-tips.

Till calmly the god of the day
    Rose with the eastern beams
Of the colours that earliest play,
    Dawning with curious gleams;
And back to my wakening will
    Hurried my soul, it seems,
But at noon and at eve it was still
    Dreaming these morning dreams.

DREAMS.

THERE are songs that sound in the silence—
   Tones from an angel-sphere
Whose harmony comes to beguile hence
   Souls whom the saints hold dear.

There are smiles that lighten the midnight
   Hours of the heart's unrest
With beautiful rays that bid night
   Cease to be all unblest.

But the songs and the smiles are only
   Born of a poor worn brain,
Whose morning is far more lonely
   Dreaming its dreams again.

COUPLETS.

One thought—two words and so the lines are
                    lengthened,
And loving souls receiving them are strength-
                    ened.

One love—two lives—that join together dearly,
While clefted heaven sheds its rays more clearly.

One soul—two worlds—till dying makes a single,
And all beatitudes forever mingle.

KISSES.

Kisses once were holy,
  Lips that gave them, chaste,
Lovers once were lowly
  Airs respectful graced.

Kisses now are common,
  Lovers true are rare,
Those who kiss a woman
  Only get a share.

Once we kissed the lasses
  For the lasses' sake,
Now we kiss for kisses—
  How the girls mistake!

WHO REMEMBERS?

Ah! who remembers
    The cinders lying
The whitened embers
    The few sparks flying
        That soon expire
When burning brightly
The next morn lightly
        The flames leap higher
        From the new fire?

Who will remember
    The frosty, snowy,
Decayed December
    That, wild and blowy,
        Undid the year,
When fresh and flowery
And summer-showery
        With days blue clear
        June joins us here?

Ah! who remembers
    The absent faces,
And who remembers
    The careworn traces
        Of tears wiped dry,

When pain departed
And happy hearted
   For hours that fly
   New friends come by?

These in their season
   Have spent their treasure
Have had their reason
   And wrought their measure
   And lived their day;
New words but bring us
What old songs sing us
   And youth grows gray
   The old, old way.

SEASONS.

Spring flowers, spring flowers, for life's young hours
Of budding promise, thriving powers;
When youth's warm heart with heaven-born reason
Unfolds like flowers that know their season.

Full corn, full corn, let that adorn
The manly hours beyond the morn;
The time was long, but now the reaping,
And time stays yet before the sleeping.

Blown leaves, blown leaves, brown autumn weaves
In garlands for the trophied sheaves;
Old triumphs through young lives are thrilling,
While dead leaves fall new buds are filling.

Bare boughs, bare boughs, let hope espouse
The dead bride-heart of broken vows;
Grim winter locks the life-tide fast,
Till breaks the new far dawn at last.

BREEZE AND BLOSSOM.

Where do all the breezes blow?
    I know, I know;
Sweeping over summer seas,
Sighing through the forest trees,
Flying over meadow leas,
    That is where they blow.

Where do all the blossoms blow?
    I know, I know;
Sweet in sunshine, fresh in rain,
In the woodland, on the plain,
In the garden and the lane,
    That is where they blow.

Where should breeze and blossom blow?
    I know, I know;
Those should blow and these should bloom,
Bearing fragrance, chasing gloom,
From the sickly city room—
    Home of want and woe

A FORSAKEN NEST.

WHEN birds with busy beaks their nests were building
   Love found a nest prepared—Love found my heart
I gave him place—to Love who is not yielding
   When sheltering Love is sharing Heaven's part?

When little birds were but half-clad with feathers
   And all their nests were full of nestlings' play,
My life was full of glad sunshiny weathers,
   For growing Love within my heart made gay

When full fledged broods flew off on wings ungrateful
   And lightly left deserted many a nest,
Love left my heart, for Love was false, deceitful—
   Yet I may not upbraid—Love was my guest!

GREAT EXPECTATIONS.

"A SHIP, a ship a-sailing,
    A-sailing on the sea,
Far wafted o'er the billows
    With precious things for me.
It is laden, heavy laden,
    With a rare and costly freight,
And it bears a royal maiden
    For whom I stand and wait."

A heart, a heart a-hoping,
    A-hoping on the strand,
And longing for the vessel
    That ne'er will reach the land.
There are scenes as fair behind it
    As ever blessed the sight,
But the hopes, the hopes that blind it
    Have stolen all the light.

A life, a life a-wasting
    As ebb the tides and flow,
'Tis bitter, bitter tasting
    The hopes that turn to woe.
Though a wreck has come for warning
    And lies upon the shore,
It is late, too late, for scorning
    The hopes that cheer no more.

EVANGELINE.

Evangeline! Evangeline!
    The dewy morn in June
That startled first those eyes of thine
    From out their baby swoon,
Gave all the brightest summer shine
Beyond the light of gem or wine,
To make their radiant spheres combine
    The sun and stars and moon.

'Tis thus thine eyes are always bright
    With lustre liquid-deep,
And blended there appears the light
    Of autumn eves that creep,
And summer noon, and winter night
And showery spring-time at its height,
To witch the dreams or wile the sight
    As one may wake or sleep.

And love, ignoring tide and time,
    Can reckon by thine eyes,
And call it morning's choicest prime
    When their long lashes rise;
A noonday in the tropic clime
To feel them bend their light sublime,
And eve, while village vespers chime,
    To see them grave and wise.

MY LADY COQUETTE.

A suitor came to a lady bright
   And wooed her on bended knee;
"I have honour and worth and a brave man's might,
   And love and a life for thee."

She spoke him soft, and she smiled him smiles,
   And gave him her flower to wear,
And sent him a quest of weary miles,
   And named his name in her prayer.

Till he said at last, "Sweetheart, sweetheart,
   I have followed thee long and well,
And the time has come when we shall not part
   Till the day of the tolling bell."

"I am sorry, my knight," the sweet voice said,
   "You have failed to understand
Our friendship was not of a kind to wed
   And another has won my hand."

Her lover laughed such a bitter laugh
   She almost feared she was wrong,
And wondered a moment of grain and chaff
   Was the difference very strong.

But he thought " What pity the queen I chose
    For the castle I built in Spain,
Was the poorest creature the whole world knows,
    The vainest of all things vain."

THE CASHIER.

A HEAP of gold and silver coin up-piling
    For a duty, sat the woman of my vow;
Madonna eyes, and lips relaxed in smiling,
    The quiet law of peace upon her brow;
Where worldly feet went back and forward filing,
    The world's lily grew beside the slough.

Must the crowning years in custom and in payment—
    The priceless—all be lavished there unprized,
And the pure fame so rich beyond all raiment
    Be worn where the vesture is despised?
Must the world, then, remain the victor-claimant
    For the fair sweet guerdon God devised?

O our Father, is it selfish, is it silly,
    To pray Thee for a portion of Thy best?
My pathway is companionless and hilly,
    I falter, I am weary and depressed;
There is comfort where it grows, in Thy lily,
    There were strength were it laid upon my breast.

TRIBUTARY.

OUTLIVING all the hopes my youth confessed,
Still toiling on, still vainly seeking rest,
A world-worn stone that never gathered moss,
Not worn enough to wear away the dross;
Unmoved by love or hate, delight or fear,
Too sad to laugh, too careless for a tear;
I deemed myself the cynic that I seemed,
And passionless as though I slept and dreamed.
But music reawakened in my mind
Emotions I forgot had been confined,
Revived the kindliness of faded youth,
And taught my old deceits an older truth.

Among a crowd of working poor one night
That filled a hall with easily won delight,
I listened, with ungratified disdain,
To song and speech and song and speech again;
At last succeeding some dull-souled harangue,
A maiden sang, and made me glad she sang.
Of all new memories that is most dear;
Like some fresh bird-voice in the dying year,
The tones recalled the voice of one I knew
When Time's white wintry rime was summer dew
And e'en the vision of the girl's clear eyes
Recalled the dreams I once thought destinies.

Like spirit lures her Beauty and her Song
Ruled each a sense and led my soul along,
While Reverence for the higher Wisdom sprang
To second birth within me as she sang:

Lovely flowers oft grow among wild weeds
   Unmarked in living and unmissed in dying;
Lovely flowers, unminded, though man needs
   A Heaven of beauty to assuage his sighing.

Lovely lives in lowliness are spent
   And no man spares a thought about the spending;
Lovely ones, though man be negligent,
   Live on, work on, God's wish awaits your tending!

Consciousness of having done its part
   Without a wasted moment's indecision,
Sweetly solaces the weary heart
   That waits the waking from this worldly vision.

Little monuments of duty done
   Are raised by many labourers unregarded;
Brighter crowns in heaven are surely won
   By those whose work on earth is unrewarded.

Thus closed the little lay she sang so well,
Thus closes all of her I have to tell;
I never saw her more, but there's a place
Within my heart all brightened by her face,
And so I write these lines to her sweet grace.

A HAWTHORN BLOSSOM.

I REMEMBER well
I wished, and she also—my Mary,—
If the thorn above us were fairy,
That I were the king and she queen
Of the elves of the thorn on the green—
    As the star fell.

And then I can tell
How I pulled two sprays of the flowers,
One was hers, one was mine: they were ours.
All the rest we left for the elves;
We only took those for ourselves
    As the star fell.

Alas! it befell
The life of her spray and mine faded,
And the scent was lost that had laded
The air, and all died that was fair!
I grieve as I think when I dare
    How my star fell.

Down into the dell
To the hawthorn I often wander;
On the grass I kneel, and I ponder;
Does she reign as an elf-queen bright
As she reigned in my heart that night
    When the star fell?

> Will the mist dispel?
> May I look on the royal splendour
> That her fairy subjects lend her?
> Shall we wish together again—
> Shall we wish together as then
> > When the star fell?

> > Or will fate compel
> My lot to be always lonely,
> Remembering happiness only?
> Will but half of our wish come true—
> If I wish again need I rue
> > That a star fell?

MAY BLOSSOMS.

The girls of Greece made merry at the marriage in the May
When the maiden bride was wedded 'mid the scent of hawthorn-spray,
While the altar flamed with torches that had thickened on the thorn,
And Athena condescended to approve the wedding-morn.

I know an Irish maiden who was merry in the May,
When we stood beneath the hawthorn on a flowery holiday.
Our hearts were wedded silently, and wafted on the wind,
Came love with all the favours he bestows when he is kind.

The vows of our betrothal made the hawthorn tree a shrine,
Where the birds, with bridal voices, sang their love and sang of mine;
The odour of the blossoms made an incense in the place,
And the sunbeams threw their radiance on her sweet wee Irish face.

A bunch of valley-lilies hung like pearls upon her
        breast,
And I held a blue-bell posy I had gathered from the
        rest;
We mixed the pearly lilies and the blue-bells, and I
        know
We mingled all our treasures, like the flowers, a year
        ago.

ODD AND EVEN.

A LADY went singing along by the sea,
The lay of a lover she carolled with glee;
The ripples of melody born from her mouth
Were wafted away on the wind to the south,
To murmur the thought in a mariner's ear—
"Though lovers be distant true love will be dear,
Though lovers be parted true love will be·near."

The lady watched long where the water and sky
Grew dim in the sundown and faint to the eye;
She thought "When the sky is so near to the sea
Should I wonder he never comes homeward to me?
With cloudland so near and the homeland so far
'Twere easy forgetting the life he might mar
In forsaking the sea to go home to a star."

The lady grew weary of pacing the sand,
And weary to death of the waves on the strand;
The marks on the beach were effaced by the tide,
The hopes faded fainter on which she relied;
Yet watched she and waited a year and a day,
While waxing how weary let lone lady say—
Some lady grown weary of lover's delay.

She stooped as she stepped on the silvery sand
And gathered the grains in her delicate hand.
She spilled them with care and she marked how they rained,
And reckoned the motes in her hand that remained.
For one he would come, and for two he would stay,
The third meant return, and the fourth spoke delay;
The last was the ninth and she cast it away.

She turned her again, and she turned to her bower—
Oh! happy the omen, and gladsome the hour—
Her lover was home, and her lover was here,
Her head on his breast, and his voice in her ear;
"Oh! love it was long!"
     "Oh! my love, I had fear!"
"Oh! love it was far!"
     "But we meet, we are near!"
And love has forgotten the leagues and the year.

THE FIRST WORD.

    An angel came
And stood beside the cradle of a child
    And spoke its name;
And near by lay the mother, sleep-beguiled,
A little space to sorrow reconciled.

    His whisper woke
The babe, who feared not at the gracious sight,
    And smiles outbroke
Upon its infant face, and sweet and bright
His answering smile made shining in the night.

    Gently he took,
As with a father's care, the fatherless,
    And let it look
On her who lay in widowed loneliness
Half-happy in some dreamed-of, dead caress.

    There he instilled
In it the knowledge of her motherhood
    Forever filled
With love, and care, and quick solicitude,
Guarding from evil, guiding into good.

  And having trained
The infant lips to voice that darling name
  That lives unstained
Beyond all speech of blessing or of blame,
He passed away in silence as he came.

  At break of day
The babe awoke upon its mother's breast,
  And as it lay
Called her that dearest name. And she confessed
The Lord is God who makes affliction blessed.

BOB AND THE STARS.

A VERSION.

WE went to the window, Bob and I,
  Someone declaring the night so fine,
And watched the wonderful winter sky
  Sparkle with frosty stars and shine,
And gleam, I thought, like the hugely high
  Cavern-roof of a jewel mine.

Bob is a small philosopher;
  I am the sire of the tender sage,
And half expect him to make a stir
  Out in the world when he comes of age,
Though as yet his infant character
  Only has reached the hopeful stage.

Bobby has curious thoughts and wise.
  Some, like himself, could stand alone,
Yet might, when they leave a father's eyes,
  Tumble down or be overthrown,
For none can properly sympathise
  With thoughts or children not their own.

Now this winter night in the starry light,
    Bob said a notable thing to me;
He asked, and his voice so low and slight
    Sounded somewhere about my knee,—
" If the bottom of heaven looks so bright,
    Father, what must the inside be?"

PAUPER AND PUP.

TRIED and true, tried and true,
Pup, stay near me, I've none but you.
Years upon years of midnight days,
Weary travel on flinty ways,
Scorching sun and searching wind,
Thunder—and lightning too, but I'm blind—
Rain, and I hear the rich complain,
Chide, as they pass, at the pouring rain,
Snow and sleet on the heartless street,
Cold and frost till one's heart is lost.
Weather and want and endless woe,
Sun and rain and wind and snow,
That's our part of it, Pup, you know.

True and tried, true and tried,
Best of my friends since Betsy died.
I am hungry and you are lean,
Skin and bones and nothing between;
Skin and bones and nothing beside—
That's how Betsy took bad and died.
Ah! you rogue, you know there's a bite
To save your life in the bag to-night;
A crust and a bone—well, it is fly-blown—
And a mite for me for bread and tea.
Then sleep for sauce with our bite and sup
Cheers our nights in the straw, my Pup,
Charity never has puffed us up.

Tried and true, tried and true,
Pup, what's left on that bone to chew?
True and tried, true and tried,
Come and lie by your master's side,
Take your share of the musty straw,
Give me hold of your poor old paw.
It seems to-night I could nearly think
Betsy made me that tea to drink;
Old Sal brewed that, the cross-tongued cat,
She's off to bed and wishing me dead,
And we're bound too, to the land of Nod;
Scorned of men in the scheme of God,
Pup, it might be better below the sod.

THE SPECTRE.

ALONG the passage, stepping light,
   She moves, half-settled, half-uncertain,
And from the window views the night
   And clutches at the velvet curtain.

The curtain with one hand she grasps,
   A missal in the other holding,
And to her breast the book she clasps
   As watching some dark scene unfolding.

The moonlight pales upon her cheeks,
   The star-light from her eyes is dying,
She shades her eyes, and turning shrieks—
"My God, the lawn, my Gerald lying."

And would alarm the house, but fails
   And falls upon the floorway swooning.
But piercing rise the dreadful wails—
   The doleful Banshee weirdly crooning.

The master and the servant soon
   The prostrate maiden there discover,
Outside, beneath the ghastly moon,
   The body lying of her lover.

For Gerald was her lover true,
   And still the people tell each other
That Brian sought to win her too,
   And wrought this deed upon his brother.

And Lady Kathleen pined and died
   For death unites what death has parted;
They say her spirit, like a bride,
   Walks calm and fair, not broken-hearted.

LILIES OF THE NIGHT.

They grow about the city
   Very beautiful and bright,
But the angels sigh for pity
   Of the lilies of the night.

Among them some are stately,
   And some are frail and slight,
But the angels pity greatly
   All the lilies of the night.

For wantons come and tear them
   Where they grow for God's delight:
They wound, but will not wear them,
   So they wither in the night.

And men are hard and trample
   On the fallen ones of night,
Though the sacred sweet Example
   Did not turn away or smite.

Father, in great compassion,
   Look from Thy throne of light;
Thou lovest Who didst fashion
   The lilies of the night.

A CHRISTMAS CAROL.

FLING forth, O stars, on Christmas night
Your radiance from the shining height,
And borrow from the Wondrous Star
The light that led the Wise Men far.

Behold, ye Magi, in the skies
The glorious company arise,
Nor let such splendour, vainly bright,
Be wasted on the sightless night.

And watch, ye shepherds, on the plain,
Attending each your pastoral train,
Till heaven's glory, once revealed,
Invades again the midnight field.

As when the sudden angel throng
Appearing, sang the immortal song—
"To God the highest glory still,
On earth, to righteous men, goodwill!"

A GREETING.

TO R. W. M'D., 23RD FEBRUARY, 1884.

WHEN Fancy with her whimsy voice
  Proclaimed your Tin-ware Wedding Day,
  Then friendship heard the Old Word say—
"Rejoice with them that do rejoice."

I give you greeting and partake
  A portion in your happiness;
  I give you greeting and address
A greeting for your lady's sake.

Two lustres of full life have linked
  Your home around with happy chains,
  While youth gives way to better gains,
And love grows more and more distinct.

'Tis yours the helpful partnerhood
  In every trouble, every need,
  The comrade heart in every deed,
The kindred hope in every good.

'Tis yours the trust of childish hands,
  The love and faith of childish eyes,
  'Tis yours to make the children wise,
To twine aright the silver strands,

'Tis yours through childhood's gradual years
    To lead them to the steeper slopes,
    Still guided by a parent's hopes,
Still guarded by a parent's fears.

And not for all has God designed
    The happiness you celebrate;
    There's many a lamp at death's dark gate
Filled full of oil, has never shined.

But God is good, we give Him praise,
    And pray we may be spared to see
    On some approaching jubilee
The children's Tin-ware Wedding Days.

IN THE TWILIGHT.

One evening when daylight was dying,
   And the stars glimmered—embers of day—
In a seat by the half open window
   I mused over years gone away.
I dwelt among beautiful shadows—
   Part sleeping and partly awake—
That rose from an ocean of fancy
   Like mists from a quiet lake.

In my age I but dream of the buried,
   The unborn was the dream of my youth,
But my dreams are now none the less pleasant
   Because they are founded on truth.
For the sadness of truth is about them,
   And the sweetness of sadness is best;
The sadness that follows our troubles
   Leaves sweetness distilled in the breast.

Than the others, one fancy more pleased me
   As I sat in the solitude then,
For it mingled the here and hereafter
   Uniting the angels with men.
A page of the scriptural story
   Was blent with the life that I knew,
Presenting a vision I wept for
   When it vanished away from my view.

A ladder of memory lifted
   From earth to the far-away clime,
Whence a glimpse of the glory of goodness
   Shone out on the darkness of time.
On the stairway an army of angels
   Came softly and solemnly down,
Whom I knew, when they gathered beside me,
   Had suffered the cross for the crown.

There was many a fervently loved one
   Had left me in trouble and tears,
There were some I had almost forgotten
   In the thronging of wearisome cares;
Yet none of them knew I was near them,
   Though some of them uttered my name;
Though evil may recognise goodness,
   Good knoweth no evil or shame.

The ladder grew dim in the sunset,
   And the fantasy faded away,
I awoke to the life that is closing
   So soon to be dead, like the day.
But I know there is ever remaining
   Some light of the love that has dawned,
To lead through the valley of shadow
   Out into the Beulah beyond

DEDICATORY.

The love of one who never spoke
   A word to her he loved the best,
Whose hidden worship never woke
   A thought in her unconscious breast;
The love of one who truly tried
   To live for her sweet sake alone,
With thought and labour sanctified
   As if herself had seen and known;
The love of one who once or twice,
   Just for a moment, held her gaze,
And gathered there a thought of price
   To cheer the darkness of the days;
The love of one who looks to stand,
   With freer friendship, face to face,
And hear her voice and touch her hand
   In the communion of God's grace;
The love of one whose grievous care
   Is calmed and tempered by that faith,
With half a cry, and half a prayer,
   Twines to her memory this wreath.

THE ROSE.

O Rose! console me now
For heaven doth allow
None else, but only thee
To witness here with me,
And keep to-night love's year long flight—
O Rose! a night of grief.

Thy life is sweet as hers
Who met the messengers
Of death and led them back
Along the brightening track,
For she knew more of heaven's far shore,—
O Rose! knew more than they.

As spotless she as thou!
God—loving—did endow
Her soul with all things pure
That here awhile endure.
But deathly sleep my love doth keep—
O Rose! a sleep of death.

O sweet and spotless Rose
Thy life draws near its close!
Sweet, sweet immaculate maid,
Her life is only stayed;
The day grows bright beyond the night—
O Rose! grows bright with dawn.

Thy beauty fades to dust
With moth-fret, mould and rust.
But hope and memory
Preserve thy sanctity,
And love's own flowers in Eden's bowers
O Rose! are flowers like thee!

ONE.

Of all the flowers at my feet
A single blossom was sweet.

Of all the birds in the tree
One alone sang for me.

Of all the starry array
One shone over my way.

But the blossom has ceased to wave;
The bird has carolled his stave;
The starlight shines on a grave!

HER GRAVE.

Let there be roses where she lies
    And let there be a lily,
And when the daylight dawns or dies
    Let nowhere be so stilly.

Let children come, of whom 'twas said—
    "Of such-like are My Father's,"
And nothing base be hither led
    While storm or sunshine gathers.

When many years forget her name
    And ancient ivies creep there,
Pray God preserve me free from blame
    And pure enough to sleep there!

EDITH'S GRAVE.

In beauty as He moulded her,
    Four years ago God gathered her—
A tender lamb, and folded her—
    An orphan child, and fathered her.

I stand beside the grave of her,
    And know that lying shattered there
Is nothing that I crave of her,
    For dust alone is scattered there.

But springing like the flowers on it,
    My thoughts spring in the heart of me;
I face the silent powers on it,
    Nor fear that death is part of me.

FADING.

She moved about with quiet tread,
  With weary steps we still remember;
The sunshine kissed her drooping head,
  Like golden leaves in sad September.
But though the chilling winds would shake,
  As yet they only breathed a warning;
And though she slept, she still would wake,
  And still we found her with the morning.

Her every act, and all her words,
  Were flowers untimely in October,
That gladdened faintly when the birds
  Grown silent, left us grave and sober.
We scarcely felt that we were glad
  To have her yet a little longer,
We dared not think that we were sad
  She did not leave us to be stronger.

We knew she was not yet to go—
  Alas! the little while was fleeting—
She fed a robin in the snow,
  She kissed us for a New Year's greeting;
But when the snowdrops trembling hung,
  Then bowed we dumbly, sorrow-laden,
The Angel of the Lord had flung
  A snow-white robe around the maiden.

JESSIE.

WHERE Jessie wrought her mission out—
    A shortened chain of April days—
And stirred my faith and slew my doubt,
    And woke the nursling Hope to praise.
There lingers yet some subtle trace
    Through all the woodland solitude,
Some wistful beauty from her face,
    Some touch of her dead maidenhood.

Her home was near, and in this glade
    She told me of the Golden Gate,
With sweet-souled counsel wisely weighed
    And faith that had not long to wait.
So have I made my journey here
    Where first I found the Golden Way,
And learned how life has less of fear
    For those who work than those who pray.

But twenty years are sown and reaped
    Since last I looked in Jessie's eyes;
The suns and rains have scorched and steeped
    The lowly bed where Jessie lies.
And from that blue between the boughs,
    And these green vistas reaching far,
Her witness, come to prove my vows,
    Arraigns me at a solemn bar,

What shall I plead ?   My years of toil,
   My charity that sought no wage,
Or that pure love that knew no soil,
   And set me this late pilgrimage ?
My God, I have not any plea,
   My secret sins profane Thy sight;
Thou art the Saviour, save Thou me,
   And lift my darkness into light.

"GOODBYE, MY WIFE."

When Love forgets to veil her eyes,
    And wisdom heals her heart,
And helps the spirit to despise
    Its baser earthborn part;
In grave glad days, all grief gone by,
    Seek, dear, the quiet place
Where in God's Acre I must lie,
    While He fulfils His grace.

And sing again the songs we sung,
    And tell the tales we told,
And all the dreams that make us young
    Will stir you as of old.
The peaceful noons and nights will pass,
    The seasons swiftly turn,
The snow will thicken on the grass,
    The ice will belt the burn.

And many a genial sun will bring
    The swallow to her nest,
And many a simple flower will spring
    Above my shrouded breast:
The daisy star in silver set;
    The dandelion's gold;
The primrose and the violet;
    The clover, honey-souled,

From May to May the years will grow,
    Each like a tender bride,
With wistful eyes and thoughts that glow,
    And life intensified.
And summers, each more brightly fair,
    With rarer charms revealed,
Inspired with every happy air
    That blows in Memory's field.

Till in a far-off fading time
    The solemn call will come,
That bids the sweet bells dull their chime,
    Earth's voices all be dumb.
Another grave will rest by mine,
    A love-enhallowed spot,
Till pity fails to read the sign
    And we shall be forgot.

Forgot!—but nameless though they go,
    While Love and Time contend,
Love's husbandmen reap what they sow,
    Love's harvest has no end.
The Lord of Life is Lord of Death,
    His winters wait for spring—
Remember, darling; breathe no breath
    Of treason to the King.

PRIMROSE DAY.

1883.

Two years have westered since the pale primroses
   Were laid to wither in the great Earl's grave.
   'Twas timid then, but now the flower is brave
To wear his memory till our history closes.

It shelters in secluded by-way places,
   A tiny thing; yet he was not too great
   To know and love it, he who loved the State,
And knew the glory spread before kings' faces.

He chose it with the subtle sapient fingers
   That wrought the world's will and controlled his time,
   And moved all chords from simple to sublime
In lordly harmony whose music lingers.

He wore it with the same familiar pleasure
   That brightens in the beggar children's cheeks
   Through all the April sunned and clouded weeks,
When wood and lane yield up their yellow treasure.

And to the service of the Sovereign-noted,
   By high and low, necessitous and rich,
   From costly garden, and from wayside ditch,
The vestal flower for ever is devoted.

He won—we wear—the pale but proud primroses,
   Pale for his death, but prouder for his life,
   Proud of the upward toil, the noble strife,
The honoured peace where that great heart reposes.

IN MEMORIAM.—LEOPOLD.

28TH MARCH, 1884.

COLD-HEARTED March's flowers of gold
   Must blanch to snow their yellow bloom
   For tribute on the untimely tomb
Of Britain's dead—Prince Leopold.

Bereaved of husband, daughter, son,
   O Queen, our thoughts are first to thee
   And yet in silence must we see
The bitter sorrow of a throne.

Young wife, amid thy sudden grief
   Thine infant's cry would make thee brave;
   But looking down upon the grave
The broken link of love is chief.

Our Scholar Prince has passed away
   Upon the verge of Easter-tide;
   And so his Royal father died
While Advent waned to Christmas Day.

The lesson is from Him who planned
   The Resurrection and the Life;
   And people, brethren, mother, wife,
Revere and love the ruling Hand.

THE FORGOTTEN POET.

WITH fragrance flown, as of a long-plucked bud,
The little song I sing with so much care,
Sweet for a day, will swoon upon the flood
Of days that will forget my song was fair.
The master-song is mighty rushing wind
Mixed with all fragrance, strong with a great breath
From cloudland, and the climes that win the mind,
And full of pulses to awaken death.
Full well I know the storm will smite my flower,
My tiny short-stemmed blossom of the sod;
But when my flower and I have lived an hour
I'll bear it on the wind away to God;
And wind and flower and spirit may adorn
Some Eden-garden where new worlds are born.

TO A LADY.

How many starlight fancies dawned and set
   And sank below the verge of surging sea
   That rolls from birth to death's eternity
In weary waves that freshen, break and fret!
What momentary visions passed ere yet
   Thy great, grave graciousness appeared to me,
   Absorbed all radiances of less degree,
And gilded all the billows of regret.
What if a sphere above me holds thy home
   Whose pathway circles higher than my course?
     A heaven-sent token and a long-sought sign
   Forever over me thy grace will shine;
Still may I pray with thee beneath one dome;
   Still trace my soul with thine to one dread Source

EDITH.

O LET me sing as clear as merry Merle
   Who does not mourn when morning is aglow
   In April-time, because his nest is low!
I see the delicate custom of the curl
That fringes on her forehead's haughty pearl,
   The ample arching brows that overgrow
   Eyes wistful-wise, not knowing all they show,
And lips where womanhood has kissed the girl.
Nobility has touched her on the brow,
   And beauty on her cheek, and by the hand
   Has led her to a throne where many bow
Before the queenship of her loveliness:
   But many stare and do not understand
   What sovereign attributes these signs express.

LOVE BEREAVED.

Death has ordained thee out of all my dreams
   And dealt me bitter check to my pursuit;
   My sunlight fails while tears are absolute,
And night falls ever chill, with scanty gleams
From clouded stars that mock the dull moon's beams.
   My summer land, long fair with flowers and fruit,
   Far cumbered lies with rotted branch and root,
In dismal fields by hopeless stagnant streams.
Death has redeemed thee out of toilsome days
   And bound thy harvest in a single sheaf,
While I went forward over saddened ways
   Whose barren progress brings but slow relief;
God aid me to the wisdom and the praise
   Of plenteous years beyond this desolate grief!

DEATH THE REVEALER.

I KNOW that death is God's interpreter:
   His quiet voice makes gracious meanings clear
   In grievous things that vex us deeply here
Between the cradle and the sepulchre.
We, gazing into darkness, greatly err,
   And fear the shrouded shadow of a fear
   Till dawn reveals the vestments of a Seer
With gifts of gold and frankincense and myrrh.
There is a mystery I cannot read
   Around the mastery I no more dread;
For love is but a heart to brood and bleed,
   And life is but a dream among the dead
Whose wisdom waits for us. God give me heed
   Till the day break and shadows all be fled!

AN APPEAL.

Release him, beauty, from the subtle bond
  Whose potency has made his bold heart meek,
  And all his hopes, but those to win thee, weak,
And those to win thee piteously despond
Though still despairingly he grows more fond!
  'Tis vain, whilst thou with dream-born tones dost speak
  Love-music, trifling with his thoughts, to seek
The happiness that braves love's magic wand.
Or since a queen, a queenly boon dispense
  And share thy heart with him who holds it rare;
  Thou hast no love whose match he cannot bring,
Thou hast no loveliness whose eminence
  Were fitter shrined than in the temple where
  He is himself the priest and offering.

TO HER WHOM IT MAY CONCERN.

Canst leave the spoil of Eden on vintage morns
   To see the waste with toil and hardship quelled ;
   Canst thou go forth as one who had rebelled,
Still innocent, and meet the bitter scorns ;
Canst take with me that journey through the thorns
   And thistle-fields, undriven—self-compelled ;
   Can Love be thy flame-swordsman, unbeheld,
With sterner heed than his who visibly warns ?
God's consecrated curse be on us, then ;
   We shall fare forth unanxious, hand-in-hand,
     To labour, prospering as our days increase,
Redeeming deserts for the world of men ;
   Spring will be with us in a winter land ;
     Grief we shall know, but also love and peace.

AN ACTRESS.

I ask but this—to mingle with the crowd
   That crowns thy beauty with a generous fame,
   And guerdons thee with such a glamorous name
The world well wonders how thou art endowed.
Thy face were not more fair if I had vowed
   A thousand vanities to vaunt the claim;
   And homage no new eminence could frame
Beyond the honour all men have allowed.
The sculptor, raptured with a perfect dream,
   Who moulds it into mimic womanhood
   And finds a genial god to grant his plea
And curb a spirit in the marble scheme,
   Could tender no more tribute if he would;
   The Hand that made thee fair most honoured thee

A PUBLIC READER.

Shamrocks were better for an Irish queen;
   Yet, being otherwhere than shamrocks grow
   One deems it not inadequate to throw
The poor best blossom from one's little green
Before the feet of her who walks serene
   Upon her highway, passing to and fro
   Among her people, leading them to know
What wise, grave, true and sweet things life may mean.
No more upon our baser bodily sight
   There breaks the rapture of the brooding Dove;
But here and there are teachers touched with might
   And filled with gifts, devoted from above;
We owe them duty, and they bring us light
   And healing leaves of Faith and Hope and Love.

OF AGE AND LOVE.

A WIFELESS grave, a childless funeral
   Are sadly yielded to the silvered head.
   The tomb looks darker for the unloved dead
To those unwitting ones who bear his pall.
They err in pity, not accounting all
   The lights on lonely pathways overshed.
   Ev'n I, the loneliest man of men unwed,
Have large sweet hopes of meetings to befall.
Here with a hand upon the latch of death
   I thank God humbly, thinking, through this gate
   Passed Edith purely; happy Marion stands
A little way within in heaven's mild breath,
   With loving Mary whom I knew too late,
   And gentle Alice, brought by the pierced Hands.

A FACE AND A FANCY.

PROCEEDING down a swarming city street,
   My footsteps fitted to the crowd's quick pace,
   A strange idea held a foremost place
Among my thoughts; but from the throng replete
With charmless presences, there chanced to greet
   My gaze one nobly intellectual face
   Which drove away my thought in instant space,
Then straightway passed among the rabble's heat.
Nor have I looked upon that face again,
   Nor ever has the thought returned to me.
   Yet if the stately brow once more I see
That now so long so longingly I've sought,
   I know at once both aims I will attain—
   I'll find it knitted, musing on my thought.

IN THE NIGHT WATCH.

The morn was bright, and prophesied a day
   That was fulfilled—that passed in facile peace
   To halt at eve, and fade with slow decrease
Through crimson sunset, gold, and twilight gray
Until the night that leadeth home the stray
   Fell darkly down and closed the little lease
   Allowed our labour to begin and cease—
The labour that is love, and loves to pray.
Now do the starbeams smile upon the few
   Who prayed and loved, and laboured all the hours
Their fields are moistened with a fresher dew,
   Methinks, the while the wakeful wanton cowers
Unfavoured. But the truth returns anew—
   That just and unjust share both shine and showers.

THE SLAUGHTER OF AGAG.

I SAMUEL, XV.

"Surely the bitterness of death is past,"
    Cried he whose safety Saul the sovereign willed
    When all the blood of Amalek else was spilled
And at his nation's grave he stood, the last.
But Samuel came with countenance overcast,
    With wrath aroused and charity all chilled,
    And there before the Lord was Agag killed,
Hewed into pieces by the Enthusiast.
Prophet of Love! whose covenant hath reversed
    The tyranny that bruised the broken reed,
Be Priest of Love and bless where all have cursed;
    Spread Thy mild rule till Hate itself be freed,
And be the King of Love whose wisdom first
    Is pure, then peaceable, and saves indeed.

IN RECOGNITION.

Brother, your lyrics pass the laws of kings
   Whose dread decrees but steeled the captive's heart
   Your home-taught lays a softer power impart,—
Love, joy, and peace, the might that mercy brings:
And, though your muse lack flight of angel's wings,
   To walk and talk with men is no mean art,
   Strong in life's straits, secure against death's dart,
Attuned to truth, foreprizing hallowed things.
Not of the mockers, nor of those who make
   Love's sacrament a feasting, passion-spiced;
Not lucre-thralled, nor cankered with the ache
   Of envy; free of almsdeed honour-priced;
Not of the world; but humbly, for His sake,
   Striving the nobler manhood after Christ.

TO CERTAIN MERCHANTS IN TORONTO.

Love is not business-like—the generous heart,
    You say, would ruin trade! Has Commerce, then,
    Declined to that low level of the men
All worlds will scorn? Must wealth depart
Without the thrift of Ananias' art,
    And base Gehazi ply a prosperous pen
    With Pharisaic wolves in Demas' den,
While Judas' thirty pieces rule the mart?
May God forbid, and give us wrath to rise
    And right these hirelings in their paltry due,
    Nor shriek to hear Czar-smitten Russia's woes
And turn deaf ears when wretched store-slaves sue
    About our feet—bondmen and maids, whose eyes
    Turn with the curse of want to you, their foes.

A CITY MINSTREL'S MUSIC.

The string-struck strains, though stained with taint
    of earth—
  Alas! that ever art betrays earth-taint—
  Were tinged with tunefulness so utter quaint,
With hazard harmony of such weird worth,
With delicacy of mild-mellow mirth,
  Commixed with tender touches of supplaint,
  In sudden minor sadness fitful-faint,
They, Orphean-born, won honour to their birth,
And claimed a crowd from out the passers by,
  And chose a chord in every crowded soul,
  That, softly docile to the spirit-stir
Gave spirit-music; which arose on high
  With each who reached his moonward garret goal
  And gave a memory to the dulcimer.

A BONNET.

(WITH APOLOGIES TO DANTE GABRIEL ROSSETTI.)

A BONNET is a woman's monument—
  Memorial of her milliner's aptitude
  To parallel her moral hardihood.
Whether on morning calls or shopping bent
Of every sumptuous fabric reverent,
  Fashioned in ribbons or with lace endued,
    She bears her own till Church and State have viewed
Its flowering crest, unrivalled—eminent.

A bonnet is a coin: the bill reveals
  How much, and to what creditor 'tis due;
Nor all the might of conjugal appeals
  Avails, when fashion offers something new;
Reason retires, Love grieves, but Woman kneels
  In mental adoration at the view.

SPARROWS.

In a fashionable gutter,
  By Chicago reckoned utter,
Two birds were heard conversing on the weather;
  And the first declared—with weight—
  That he'd like to know the date
When refrigerated sparrows paired together.

He believed that Valentine
  On the other side the brine,
Had decided on the middle of the month,
  "But it seems," he said, "to me
  That the period here must be
Deferred to February thirty-oneth."

"I concede," said number two,
  "The justice of your view,
For where's the good in getting up a wedding,
  When you'd search for half a day
  For a mouldy bit of hay,
Or a feather that was thawed enough for bedding

"I have bought a marriage license,
  And of course I have a high sense
Of my duty to the warbler who consented,
  But one needn't scoop a nest
  In a chunk of ice and rest
With the notion she'll be more than half contented

"Despair has turned me black:
  I have shivers down my back,
And my tail is little better than an icicle;
  It's a skeleton I am,
  And a feather-coated sham,
For I'm skinnier and leaner than a bicycle!"

  Just then came flying by
  A third with merry cry—
"The thaw has started in to-day for keeps!"
  And they cocked their little tails,
  For their courage never fails,
And the wedding-cards are out among the Cheeps.

*　*　*　*　*　*　*　*

  Little buccaneering birdie
  You are stout of heart and sturdy:
There is something of the Saxon in your pluck;
  And I think you may suggest
  From that tangle-town, your nest,
That we must not trust our happiness to luck.

  You have conquered every storm
  And your breast is throbbing warm
For the building and the brooding soon to be;
  Who fashioned you will feed you,
  Who laid your path will lead you,
On the thoroughfare, the house-top, or the tree.

KATE BERRY.

I'D have thought it more romantic
   Had we been some birthdays older,
Or if you'd been less pedantic,
   And I just a trifle bolder.
But you looked like such a maiden
   As one would not dare to flutter,
With your bag of school-books laden,
   And the task I heard you mutter.
      So I only sat and looked,
         And you only sat and read,
         And we could not be rebuked
           For anything ill-bred.

I'd have though it more romantic
   Had the scene been somewhat finer,
Were it crossing the Atlantic
   Cabin passage on a liner;
On a stage-coach even, sitting,
   As true lovers long ago did,
Or a ferry-boat were fitting,
   Some fine morning, overloaded.
      But we met as fate preferred,
         In a vulgar railway-train,
         Where the carriage was a third,
           And the seats were hard and plain.

I'd have thought it more romantic
  Had there been an introduction,
But though courtiers may go frantic,
  Fate is deaf to all instruction.
Yet while one must live politely,
  Be it ne'er so inconvenient,
And as custom binds so tightly
  Luck might sometimes be more lenient.
    Still—by a curious hap—
      I saw your pretty name,
    On the bag, below the flap,
      When you opened up the same.

And in Rob Roy's part of Stirling,
  remember where to drop at,
For the railway now goes whirling
  Where the coaches used to stop at.
I can fancy what your home is,
  What the garden and the gate is,
Neat and sweet as honey-comb is,
  Trim with roses and clematis.
    And you might be at the door,
      Or a window open wide,
    And apparelled as before
      With a maiden's modest pride.

But I'd think it most poetic
  Should I find you some vacation,
Seeking intercourse æsthetic
  In a classic compilation:

But the ancient slightly hateful
   When you wanted to be merry,
And a modern bard more grateful
   To your taste—sweet Katie Berry.
      Ah! my Katie—bonnie Kate—
         If we ever meet anew
      And it be not all too late
         I'll pluck heart enough to woo.

IN LODGINGS.

How Alice would smile if she saw me recline
    In my easiest chair to look over my pictures,
And pause at one portrait that isn't divine
    Yet doesn't permit any critical strictures.
She would say what a fool I was doting on this,
    Till my arm round her waist became very ecstatic—
Now you'd almost suppose it was naughty to kiss
    When she wants to be very dogmatic.

If Alice were here she would probably smile
    At my poor little wofully modest interior;
She'd compare it with quarters I've had, and the style
    Is decidedly shabby and wholly inferior.
But one cannot live always in clover and June,
    Nor while making a fortune abide in a palace
I'm content to be thrifty to-day for the boon
    Of spending to-morrow with Alice.

I have rented a room in the rear of the flat,
    And the window looks out on a desolate entry,
Where midnight discovers the jubilant cat,
    And a dolorous dog keeping vigilant sentry;
Yet the prospect is not at all bad—when you think—
    You can see a few far-away stars when they're shining,
And the moonlight bestows an occasional blink,
    With suggestions of clouds with a lining.

There's an almanac stuck on the back of a door,
    And a map of the city is pinned to another;
Here a photograph hangs of my *colleen asthore*,
    And one over there they say favours my mother;
Here's a table with trumpery, papers, and books;
    Here's a basin and highly unclassical chalice
In exchange for the brooks and the flies and the hooks
    And the last summer's angling with Alice.

My trio of chairs might make room for some more
    If my drawers and my trunk were a thought less
        capacious;
If the bed didn't straddle all over the floor
    You might come to believe the apartment was
        spacious.
But the walls are not distant enough to be cold,
    Nor to lend the enchantment that tickles the poet,
And at least if the place be a den—I'm consoled
    That there isn't a grumbler to know it.

Some other folks live in the chambers around,
    For I hear their alarums' importunate warning;
You can study the punctual paganish sound
    Through deplorably barbarous hours of the morning.
But that is as near as these strangers attain
    To arousing a thought of goodwill or of malice;
The day has its labour, the hours that remain
    I lavish on thoughts about Alice.

LADY MYRTLE DANCED A WALTZ.

My heels are playing on the pavement,
   My wits rebel and play me false,
For fancy o'er an old enslavement
   Plays, while the soldiers play a waltz.
And so I cannot but remember—
   The music puts me in its debt—
A ball-night in a white December,
   A tennis-lawn with May-dew wet.

'Tis strange that after many seasons
   We like to see the old dim stars,
And spite of half a hundred reasons,
   Gaze from behind the old cell-bars.
My heart's a graveyard; often weeping
   My hopes and thoughts sit there in black,
For there my dearest loves are sleeping,
   All dead in early youth, good lack!

Love ratifies no vain averment
   Or I would show you, face to face,
Recalled once more from long interment,
   A resurrection full of grace;
That you from phantom feet the lightest,
   From fairy forms might choose the best,
From brilliant dames select the brightest—
   And yield what no one will contest.

You could not then conceive it curious
  A soldiers' band should make me dull—
You think my sentiment is spurious ?—
  My friend, you're weighted with a skull.
Hope waits on consciences that suffer,
  Hearts soften that are hard as stick,
The thinly skinned may yet grow tougher,
  But nothing saves a head that's thick.

I'll call on someone else to measure
  The merits of my dreamland bride,
Or at my own abundant leisure
  Discuss the maiden and decide.
They called her clever, sweet, and pious,
  I saw it shining in her eyes;
But evermore the gods deny us
  The wives we think we most could prize.

I heard her sing a glorious ballad,
  They told me that she studied hard,
I helped her to the chicken salad
  With feelings of profound regard.
And never spoke to her thereafter,
  But heard of her at distant whiles,
For where she came came merry laughter,
  And where she was were pleasant smiles.

I call them flowers, the passion fancies
  That cumber one with needless cares,
The social roses, fashion pansies—
  Who likes may call them weeds or tares,

Love's acre is extremely fertile
   In immortelles that last for hours,
But here's a sprig of real Myrtle
   To grace my bunch of passion flowers.

AN EMPTY PROGRAMME.

One guest will claim
   No dance to-night;
No charming dame
   Can charm him quite.
From square to round
   The music runs,
He likes the sound—
   The dance he shuns.
A lily stoops,
   A rose attracts,
A wall-flower hopes,
   A willow acts;
"He is a clown!"
   "He cannot dance!"
The maidens frown,
   And look askance.
"What brings him here?"
   Asks curious Belle;
Suppose, my dear,
   For news to tell.
His eyes and ears
   Are chroniclers,
And someone hears
   Of all occurs.

A distant hand
   And darling face,
His thoughts command
   In this gay place.
The world may smile,
   He smiles at heart,
And for awhile
   He dwells apart.
In after days
   The world will blow
Some feather-phrase—
   "I told you so!"—
From tongue to tongue,
   And make believe
His heart was hung
   Upon his sleeve.
But not to-night
   The world divines
What love may write
   Between the lines.

CUPID AND CUPIDITY.

There are blessings still in store
   When we're desperate of the least;
I have fallen in love once more
   Though I thought I quite had ceased.
Once again I feel the ache,
   And the yearning and the flame,
And the thrill you can't mistake
   When you hear the lady's name.

She's so positively rich
   Quite a host of fellows vow
That she ought to settle which
   She proposes to endow.
But her heart's a secret shrine
   Where a magic fountain drips;
She would scorn to waste love's wine
   On their avaricious lips

I exhibit ignorance
   Of her father's stocks and shares,
And when people talk finance
   I assume superior airs.
Yet with wariness and wile
   Though my wits are well combined,
Still her red lips do not smile,
   Nor her pretty eyes look kind.

Every hope and wish beside,
   Every prospect, faint or large,
I'd forego if she'd confide
   Her dear future to my charge.
For love little recks of thrift
   When youth's passion gathers heat;
All my life in one great gift
   I would lavish at her feet.

She has self-assertive ways
   And her plans are all her own,
What she purchases or pays
   Is her business alone.
But upon her haughty brow
   Other dealings will appear;
There is many a happy vow
   To be whispered in her ear.

Not in politics profound
   She is clever in the house;
She will stand upon her ground
   During rumours of a mouse.
And she never faints of fright
   When a chimney goes on fire,
While a thunderstorm at night
   Is a thing we both admire.

She has principles of dress
   Which respect the latest code,
But she quite avoids excess
   And abhors the waspish mode.

She has never heaped her head
  With a trophy of the chase;
She objects to brilliant red,
  And despises modern lace.

With a talent quite unfeigned
  She is court and kitchen wise;
And phenomenally trained
  She can cook and criticise.
She could bake you white or brown,
  And the servants proudly say
You must tie her sponge-cake down
  Lest it rise and float away.

For good music and high art,
  For the ball-room and the street,
Growing native in her heart
  That rare blossom—Taste—you meet.
She detests (I hate it too)
  All society veneer,
And the way she looks it through
  Is distractingly severe.

While the flowers that seek the sun
  Are the soonest flowers to fall,
Fruit the hardest to be won
  Is the sweetest after all.
So I humour her conceits
  And endeavour not to vex;
Could you win her—Hope repeats—
  You could sign your name to cheques.

TRIOLET.

Love has such a lot to say,
   Christmas says it in a word,
Half in earnest, half in play,
Love has such a lot to say
Sorrow sets a holiday
   Comforted with all she heard.
Love has such a lot to say
   Christmas says it in a word.

A CHRISTMAS CARD.

In the days of Methusalem, ages ago,
Our grandfathers revelled in ice and in snow;
But we've varied all that, it was really too slow,
And we relegate such to the mild Esquimaux.

A fig for the grievance of winterless weather,
As long as good friends can be gathered together
With spirits as light—hearts as warm—as a feather
And Time tugging gently his end of the tether.

Let the season be frosty, or windy, or wet,
The claims of old Yule we can never forget,
And we'll honour the holly as happily yet
As our ancestors did when they merrily met.

Then here's to the turkey, the goose or the gander,
To the blazing plum-pudding dyspeptics all slander,
To the mistletoe bough, and—what toast can be
    grander?—
The health of King Christmas, the Revel Commander.

BABY NEW YEAR.

ANOTHER baby-year is born,
As everybody heard this morn,
As fine a child as ever came,
Though every father says the same.
Just see him smile, and how he cries,
And how he dreams with open eyes,
And how he shuts them close to sleep
And opens them again to weep.
A little commonplace—perhaps!
But look in other people's laps
And find a better baby there
Than this that just begins to stare;
Get one will grow just half as fast
And show such shoulder breadth at last!
He'll live as much in one short day
As all the world at once, they say.
We mean to give him lots of school
And teach him not to be a fool;
And so when April comes he'll know
His way about the raree-show.
He'll sentimentalize in May,
And wander through the fields all day,
And doubtless—not a bit too soon—
He'll marry somebody in June.

We hope he'll make a name for work
When August apple-orchards smirk,
And fill the harvest garners up,
And brin September's cider-cup.
And if the rest of life he spends
Hobnobbing with his early friends
We'll never speak a word's complaint—
Besides he'll never bear restraint.
And more, and this is truly bad,
He'll be a glutton from a lad,
And surfeiting on Christmas pie
Before next New Year comes, he'll die!

A JANUARY THAW.

O GREAT Canadian winter,
   King Frost and Ice and Snow,
Your sceptre's but a splinter,
   Your robes are all aflow.
You that were bright and bracing
   Now all collapsed and raw
Confess defeat when facing
   A January thaw.

Approach! our latest rubbers!
   Depart! our overshoes!
Aye! scoff, ye southern lubbers
   Our sealskins we refuse.
Umbrellas wave defiant
   From every shivering paw
That shakes to meet the giant—
   The January thaw.

Where does the snow-shoe wander?
   Where does the skater glide?
And is that ruin yonder
   Our best toboggan slide?
Ah! let the street-car hide us
   Upholstered deep in straw,
Ere destiny o'er-ride us—
   The January thaw.

My vertebræ are melting,
   I nurse a wild catarrh,
The rain without is pelting—
   How hopeless sleigh-rides are!
Does Kate, I wonder whether,
   Feel stupid as a daw—
All underneath the weather—
   The January thaw?

VALENTINE.

A YEAR or more ago I met
    A maid whose eyes were blue,
And when I see her big blue eyes
    I always think of you.

Pretty fair brown hair she has
    In curls that fringe and flow;
It would, if I'd a lock of it,
    Remind me of you so.

Her hands are small and white and soft,
    And kind in granting prayers,
And on her gemmed and gentle hands
    Your size of glove she wears.

Her dainty little feet are shod
    With dainty little shoes;
Like yours they trample underfoot
    Men's egotistic views.

She is a little fairy from
    A broken mould of fate;
If we should lose you all the world
    Has not her duplicate.

Of course I got her photograph,
    And cheaper than a song;
A friend of mine had one of you—
    I robbed him—was I wrong?

And now you guess the riddle, dear,
    You know you're both the same,
And I admire you twice as much
    As any other flame.

FATE, THE MILKMAN.

My Fate's a wicked dairy-man
   Who sells me skim and charges cream,
Puts "Human-kindness" on his can,
   And cold pump-water on my dream.

With deprecatory pretence
   He begs his dues like other prigs—
My time, my labour, and my pence,
   And steals my tit-bits for his pigs.

I asked him why the milk I buy
   Is worse than theirs who dress in silk,
But craftily he made reply—
   "I furnish them with asses' milk!"

I'd gladly change, but where I dwell
   He quite controls his branch of trade;
He is an anchorite as well
   And does not keep a dairy-maid.

O Milkman Fate! these many years
   Your human-kindness mocks my thirst;
Your sweetest milk is salt with tears
   And on such food my hopes are nursed.

EYE WISDOM.

When man relies on woman's eyes
    His destiny to shew forth,
Let him beware the black arts there,
    The treachery and so forth.
Each dear deceit seems oh! so sweet,
    Desirable and truthful,
The fools make haste deep joy to taste
    And suck a bitter toothful.

Eyes raven black may well bring back
    One's dread of that dark omen,
And eyes of grey will soon betray
    One's credence in a woman.
Soft eyes of brown will reap renown
    For falsehood with the bluest,—
In every pair lies love's despair,
    The newest are the truest.

The Chinese play looks very gay
    With lamps of colored paper,
When every flame burns just the same
    Upon a tallow taper.
So women's eyes, if men were wise,
    Are lanterns highly tinted,
A tallow kind of light behind,
    And tallow rather stinted.

ONE OF THE LEFT.

My rival was wealthier far,
    And his face had a handsomer cast;
He could smoke a delicious cigar,
    I was morally strong—he was fast.

He had jilted two earlier girls,
    I discountenance people who flirt;
When I called him a swine among pearls,
    He called me a swine among dirt.

He always threw dust in her eyes,
    While I strove to enlighten her youth;
He told her all manner of lies
    While I manfully stuck to the truth.

When I asked her at last to be mine
    I found he had asked to be hers;
He had promised her France and the Rhine—
    I, the blessings a true heart confers.

I offered her love and a home,
    But the programme omitted to draw;
My music was paper and comb,
    While he blew his horn with *eclat*.

Now I'm fully recovered from pique
    And my heart is as whole as a bung,
But she hasn't her sorrows to seek
    And he's sick of the sound of her tongue.

Though marriage may be a success—
    A point on which few are agreed—
In courtship—the primary mess,
    To fail is good fortune indeed.

TO BEAUTY ASLEEP AMONG LILIES.

By Swinburne Jones.

Meagre measure of a garment garbs the dreaming dream divine,
Brood of beauties that like stars in stately constellation shine,
Face of fancy, flower of fancy, the adroitest feat of fate,
Figure fraught with fascination, form that Hate alone could hate,
Angel ankles, members matching, fair as this could nothing be,
Sight of sights uncited hereto, soul-sweet-surfeiting to see.

THE PEANUT BALLADS.

(To be read in the Belfast vernacular.)

I. THE PEANUT STAND.

There's a mighty tidy city at the foot of the Cave Hill,
Where my father was a hackler in the Edenderry Mill,
And my uncle was an Islandman, a rivetter to trade,
And sweated on the longest keels and speediest ever laid;
For they say the White Star passes all the flags that sail the sea,
And every Nic and Tic of them was built on Belfast Quay.
But there's far too many boys at home, so in a foreign land,
That's how I came to settle at a peanut stand.

I landed in Toronto, and I walked about for days,
Till my pocket was as empty as a nest where nothing lays;
I went without my tea one day, and breakfast, and for lunch
I found a little picking on a bad banana bunch.

I tightened up my braces like you tighten up a drum
And I felt a sight too hollow only sucking at my
    thumb,
But my chance came round immediately as if it had
    been planned,
And I'm making dollars steady at my peanut stand.

I was coming round a corner when I lit upon a fight,
A big man on a little one which never yet was right,
The big one full of liquor till he couldn't hold his
    views,
And the wee one full of nothing but the bones he
    couldn't lose.
'Twas a dirty-fisted Dago with a black-a-visted face,
And a pair of yellow peepers would have frightened
    you from grace,
But the big one stole some peanuts and the Dago held
    his hand,
Till I helped to cure the trouble at the peanut stand.

If you lived upon the Lagan you'd have muscles in
    your skin,
And sure all the good Belfast in me just rose and
    waded in;
So he left the little Dago but I clipped him in the neck,
And his liquor lost its virtue when I dropped him on
    the deck.
He rose and looked me over, and he swore what he
    would do,
But he thought too long about it, and the crowd
    allowed him through.

Well, sir, the little Dago up and offered me his hand,
And that's how he got a partner at the peanut stand.

Now this small Italian Dago-man was old, and thin,
    and done,
Or it wasn't in his nature for to treat me like a son,
But as soon as I let on that I was starving for a meal,
He set me up a dinner would have done for Lord
    O'Neill.
And from that I got to helping him, and wheeling
    home his cart,
And for all he was a heathen, yet it wasn't to the heart;
So we worked along together, till the snow fell on the
    land,
And left us next to powerless at the peanut stand.

He hadn't one to own him, or to call upon in need,
And we didn't have a deal of crack through differing
    in breed,
But we got along harmonious till the frost got in his
    chest,
And he lay down weak one evening, and was plainly
    near his rest.
He slept awhile in quiet, and I thought he'd last till
    light,
But he took a turn towards morning, and sat up
    most cruel white,
And I saw the life was leaving him like water leaving
    sand,
As he told me how I'd have to keep the peanut stand.

He maybe would have liked a priest to put him on
    his way,
But I couldn't leave him lying there alone in death's
    dismay;
So I got a little crucifix he kept among his clothes
And thought how Roaring Hanna used to preach to
    love your foes
When the Teagues were extra bitter at the Sabbath
    scholars' trips,
And for all I was an Orangeman I held it to his lips.
The Lord has many a way it seems of reaching out
    His hand,
And the creature never fretted for his peanut stand.

Good luck has kept near hand me since the poor old
    being died,
And I hope it helps to comfort him wherever he may
    bide.
I'm doing bravely since although a Papist gave the
    start,
And now I've put in apples and a pony to the cart.
It won't be very long before I open up a store,
So one thing brings another when you're looking out
    for more,
For I wrote to Pollie Rea I was her sweetheart to
    command,
And she says she'll share the profits of the peanut
    stand.

II. THE PEANUT WEDDING.

There's far too much advice about the way we ought
    to marry,
  For no matter what you follow likely lands you in
    a hole,
And heaps of decent couples that are going to old
    Harry,
  Are spoiled by friends' advice, upsetting notions,
    and the Bowl.
For advice, I listen freely, and I do what I think pro-
    per,
  And I never drank that much but I could keep my
    powder dry;
As for pride, I take a fortune for a fortune—gold or
    copper—
  And for rank—well, Pollie thinks there's none can
    stand with Sam McKay.

Some folks believe this life is only one of many
    threaded
  On the strands of life and death like sleep and
    waking day by day,
And the friends that we have gathered, and the wives
    that we have wedded,
  Just old acquaintance newly dressed in fashionable
    clay.

If it's true that we're rewarded here for foregone
    deeds and doings,
  'Twould be only fair and square and make it worth
    your while to try,
'Twould explain a lot to know we're only supping our
    own brewings,
  And maybe tell why Pollie Rea is Mrs. Sam McKay.

Her friends were in a better way of doing than my
    father's,
  And the time I saw her first was running barefoot
    on the street,
I told my ma I'd marry her, but all I got was
    "Blathers,
  "A boy like you had better think of working for
    his meat."
Thirteen I was; the last five years, my uncle had me
    schooling
  At the Ballymena Model till it happened him to
    die;
I had to leave it for Belfast, but spite of lots of fooling
  There was only Harry Kennedy ahead of Sam
    McKay.

I used to go to church to see her sitting there fornenst
    me,
  So she grew from eight to twenty and I came to
    twenty-five;
And though I sparked a lot of girls and had it laid
    against me,

They never altered Pollie Rea with all they could
    contrive.
Of course she was a teacher and a good deal set above
    me,
But she went with me to Bangor once—my heart
    was in the sky—
And round by Ballyholme she let it out she'd always
    love me,
And she said she'd do her best to make a man of
    Sam McKay.

Old country notions have it you must marry in your
    station,
Be it teacher and mechanic, or a princess and a
    peer,
So with that and slack employment, I gave up my
    situation,
And with Pollie's love and photograph I emigrated
    here.
Peanuts and luck befriended me, and after five years'
    saving,
I sent her home her passage, and for all she'd want
    to buy,
Then I met her on the "Sarnia" with her handker-
    chief a-waving,
And the Montreal good man and *her* soon married
    Sam McKay.

We came down the Thousand Islands in the steamer
    to Toronto

And I left the store to Billy for the balance of the
    week ;
I thought we'd see Niagara, because I knew she'd
    want to
Before she settled down for good among the kitchen
    reek.
We saw the whole belongings round that water
    always pouring,
And I couldn't sleep with listening to it never run-
    ning dry,
And thinking of the waste of it, the dashing and the
    roaring,
. 'Twould turn my head to live at it as sure as I'm
    McKay.

But Pollie kissed me every night for bringing her to
    see it;
    The rainbow on the water-mist she said was worth
        God's while;
The water was a wonder, but the Finger that could
    free it
    Was the marvel far beyond them all—Niagara or
        the Nile!
I think she has more mind than *me*, or had more
    exercising,
    For I'd rather hear a katy-did or see a strange bird
        fly,
Than spend my time with water-falls, and things as
    much surprising,
    But that makes us complementary, says Mrs. Sam
        McKay.

The places Captain Webb was in the guides were
    bound to show us
  Till I wondered what they talked about before his
    foolish vow;
And we drove to see the Whirlpool boiling far away
    below us
  Where I thought I saw a dog was drowned, but sure
    it was a cow.
And now we've seen it end to end I'm glad we're home
    in quiet,
  And settled in our own wee house with not a tear
    to cry,
Away out near the Woodbine where land's cheap
    enough to buy it,
  And friends are always welcome warm to Mrs. Sam
    McKay.

III. A PEANUT LEGEND.

Young Hezekiah Mee fell deep in love with Ethel
    Murphy,
  So William Dander told me on the Island last July,
We were lying snug and shady where the grass was
    soft and turfy,
  And the Bay was boiling over, and the boats were
    in a fry.
Now Dander beats the old one when it comes to
    telling stories,
  And he'll talk a month of Sundays if you let him
    smoke his clay;
Och! he's great about his travels, or on Ireland's
    ancient glories,
  And you never met his equal yet when day-li'-gone*
    is gray.

Well, Miss Ethel was an orphan, and an heiress,
    William started,
  And as lovely as Queen Vashti, and by all accounts
    as proud,
But Hezekiah doted on her, not a bit downhearted,
  Because he was no more to her than any in the
    crowd.

    *Day-light gone, *i.e.*, twilight.

He wasn't too well favoured, and he wasn't very clever,
   And thirty bob a week was every penny of his pay,
But with managing he spruced himself and did his best endeavour,
   And joined the Linen Hall*, and read the books in section K.

He came no speed at all at all in meeting with the lady,
   And it's very well he didn't, for he'd just have got a snub,
But he kept on saving money and one fine and happy pay-day
   He bought a brand new bicycle and joined the Richmond Club.
And after that by day and night he dreamt on tracks and training,
   Till the joggling of his legs would knock the blankets all astray,
And he'd start awake and hurry, be the weather dry or raining,
   To be out and on the cinder-pad before the screek of day.

He knew she wouldn't speak to him unless he could be famous,
   And he never could catch up to that unless it was on wheels,
But he thought he'd learn Miss Ethel he was not an ignoramus
   When he owned the champion muscles and the smartest pair of heels.

   *Reading-room and Library.

The spring of eighty-four it was he started first at
　　racing,
　At the Easter sports in April he was premier of
　　the day;
There had been a lot of preaching that athletics were
　　debasing,
　"And I'll debase the record," Hezekiah said, "in
　　May."

His form was something wonderful, his spurting led
　　the fashion,
　And nothing in Belfast could touch him one to fifty
　　miles;
But still he was the victim of an agitating passion,
　And as far away as ever from Miss Ethel Murphy's
　　smiles.
So he notified the Club and they appointed a com-
　　mittee
　To time him on the morning of the twenty-fourth
　　of May,
And they gathered bright and early, at the morning
　　prime so pretty,
　With Dander's big chronometer to regulate the play.

The Lagan ran like silver in the morning sunlight
　　shining,
　And the great trees wore their greenest of the fresh
　　and dewy spring,
The Ormeau Park is beautiful, but fair beyond divining
　In the first rich life of summer ere the Mayfly takes
　　its wing.

An even mile the race track ran, through planes and
    elms and beeches,
  And the Captain had his ticker ready waiting Mee
    to mount,
When a tall, dark man came forward, and an oilcan
    out he reaches,
  And says, "Just you try this oil here; it will help
    your wheels to count."

Well, Hezekiah oiled again, ball-bearings, head and
    pedals,
  And thanked the tall dark stranger and remounted
    his machine,
While the Captain looked annoyed, the way you look
    at one that meddles,
  But gave the word and started him while interest
    got keen.
"Three-forty-three," cried Dander as he closed the
    first lap easy,
  "He needs a man to speed him," cried the Bugler
    with conceit;
"He's waiting on his wind," said one; "I noticed he
    was wheezy,"
  But walking off, half-laughing, said the stranger,
    "It's the heat."

The second mile was better; said the Captain "Three-
    eleven,"
  As he swept down round the corner past the crowd
    upon the grass,

And they cheered him loud and hearty at the third
" Two-fifty-seven,"
And they saw his teeth set steady as they gave him
room to pass.
The fourth one finished " Fifty-two," and gathering
round the ticker,
They wondered as they watched him spurting down
the long, straight track,
To lose him at the turn among the trees, till quick
and quicker,
And humming like a bee among the bushes, he came
back.

" Two-forty-one," they yelled and screeched, as on he
went still faster ;
" He'll whack the record hollow if he's only fit to
stay."
Some cautious fellows muttered they were feared of
a disaster,
" His wheel might buckle under him ; the rubber
might give way."
But the sixth mile reeled below him, and the record
went to pieces
As the seventh one was finished with a cheer that
tore the air ;
" Two-twenty-eight and game for more. Each lap
the pace increases."
Said the Captain, " Mr. Bugler, you can speed him
if you care."

The eighth and ninth went higher, and the tenth just
        touched two minutes;
  Then even William Dander thought they'd pretty
        near enough,
And the whole lot got that quiet they could hear a
        pair of linnets
  That were singing right behind them, and the
        Captain tore his cuff,
But on went Hezekiah, never slacking, never minding,
  But whizzing round the corners sharp at forty-five
        degrees,
Till they noticed at the thirteenth lap, as harder he
        came grinding,
  A sort of steam behind him on the light May morn-
        ing breeze.

A mist like thin tobacco reek, uncanny and mysterious,
  And his eye was fiery flaming as he passed them
        once again,
" We must stop him," then said Dander; "Yes," the
        Captain said, " It's serious;
  It looks like he was melting since he finished off
        the ten."
But he flew ahead still faster at a rate beyond all
        telling;
  They heard the spokes revolving with a gruesome
        sort of scream,
As sweeping, whirling past them, some terrific force
        impelling,
  He turned the eighteenth corner in a drifting cloud
        of steam.

But when he came the next time there was nothing of
    the vapour,
  The crying noise the spokes had made had faded
    clean away,
His face seemed half-transparent with a look of tissue
    paper,
  And his flannels looked like gossamer or cobweb
    silver grey.
But his eyes kept burning, burning, though he seemed
    so light and airy,
  As he did the mile a minute and went by them like
    a flash;
And then the Bugler fainted, as it seems, to be con-
    trary,
  And falling on two bicycles, upset them with a crash.

'Twas somehow then they lost him with the fainting
    and the flurry,
  Some said he took the Lagan Village, some the
    Ormeau Gate;
But they got the Bugler better and went homeward
    in a hurry,
  And agreed to keep it quiet, and they never ride
    out late.
Yet the queerest thing about it all was what they
    heard at dinner;
  That morning, very suddenly, Miss Ethel Murphy
    died.
And Dander says it makes him creep and feel a
    bigger sinner
  To think of what he saw of Hezekiah's phantom ride.

IV. PEANUT MEMORIES.

Did you ever feel that lonesome like that nothing could content you,
  With your heart all swollen, rolling like a river-tide at flood,
Till the weëst things that happened would that fidget and torment you
  The sight of them you fed and clothed would poison all your blood?
I felt like that last year in March one evening after *quetting*,
  'Twas the seventeenth of Ireland coming set me thinking long,
A hen on a hot griddle never equalled me for fretting
  So I took a dander after dark to clear up what was wrong.

The stars were bright—so clear and bright—I couldn't look below them,
  And I never felt the frost-wind blowing bitter through my coat,
For they every one kept shining down and asking did I know them,
  Did I mind at Ballymena on the fairy-forayed Moat?

Did I mind them? Could I think of any other mor-
   tal notion,
  With nothing changed about them but the boy that
     saw them shine;
If the Hebrews turned their noses up at Canaan after
   Goshen
  Sure an Irish heart may hanker for the home ayont
     the brine?

I was homesick, that's the long-come-short, and five
   good miles and *farder*
  I travelled up and down before I got a bit of peace,
For a man that has a wife and wean to shift for takes
   it harder
  When his feelings turn and gabble at him like a
     flock of geese.
And still one great big star kept shining, shining clear
   and glorious,
  And a voice it had kept asking with a tongue that
     wouldn't tire,
I could hear it still and quiet though the night-wind
   blew uproarious—
  "Do you think your mother's happy by her lonely
     kitchen-fire?"

My heart rose like a boat upon a surging crest of
   sorrow
  And sank away to nothing in a trough of sore
     despair;

I had no use to live at all; I'd give the Lord's to-morrow
  To be just a wee wee boy again beside my mother's chair.
The glow of later summers touches childhood with such gilding
  That all the gold of life between looks dark and dull and dim;
And manhood's chant, and labour's lay, the songs of fortune-building,
  Sound harsh to ears that hear again the far-off children's hymn.

I was back again in Lorimerstown, a barefoot wean of seven,
  Winding bobbins, dropping praties, dibbling plants, or mixing swill,
Or free by law or license to get one whole day from heaven,
  Going wading, catching spricklies at the foot of Church's hill.
Or chasing things with picture wings in spite of regulations
  Through clover-fields and corn-fields, pulling cress at Vincent's well,
Or finding nests and scaring rabbits over Young's plantations,
  And clodding stones and climbing, doing things I durstn't tell.

And coming home worn out at last, with clothes in
    want of mending,
  And meeting mother, shamefaced for the clabber
    on them thick;
And seeing father weaving as I left him, only bending
    A little more above the heddles, looking white and
      sick;
And eating fadge and soda-bread, and washing in the
    bucket,
  And sleeping somewhere, soon and snug, with
    mother singing low—
We get the balance seldom but that night the star-
    shine struck it,
  And my heart was wrenched to learn the price a
    man must pay to grow.

Yet life is well worth living and I hurried home to
    Pollie,
  And she wasn't vexed a bit because I left her feel-
    ing blue;
She's sense and comfort always when I feel a twinge
    of folly,
  And life's a great investment when your wife has
    wit for two.
I told her all I thought and how I wanted baby's
    grannie
  To come across in summer-time and stay with us
    awhile;
How proud she'd be to get the chance to nurse our
    own wee mannie,
  Nor ever interfering in the husband's mother's style.

And Pollie said she didn't want to go back home this
 long time,
 But she'd dearly love to see a face just fresh from
  old Belfast,
When the year had spread to spring-time, grown to
 flower-time, turned to song-time,
 She would like to look in Irish eyes and talk about
  the past.
And that's how mother's visit in the summer-time
 was settled,
 She made no bones about it when we wrote for her
  to come;
True love goes round the world, she said, and mother's
 love's high mettled,
 And the older still the abler, and the Lord puts
  down the sum.

V. A PEANUT ROMANCE.

It's William Dander tells the crack of Billy McIlvane,
   Though every man and child from Portglenone to Cushendall
Kenned Billy well and worthy, since the time he was a wean
   Till the day they took him coffined from Ahoghill Orange Hall.
For Dander says he beat the heathen god upon the fife,
   And every Twelfth the lodges had him aye in great request;
It was wonderful to hear him, but it took away his life,
   And the tune was never made could pay a man to spoil his chest.

But Dander says the fifing never hurted him at all,
   'Twas the wetting, and the damp and cold, and getting chilled at night;
He says that Billy told him when he took too sick to crawl
   How misfortunate a thing it was, and wanted it told right.

'Twas one of **Billy's** ways to go round showing how to play
  To a wheen of fellows living all about the country side,
And they had him at lint-pullings, and at Orange Balls for pay,
  For 'twas well-beknown his **fifing** beat all fiddling far and wide.

He was used to coming home at any hour you'd see the stars,
  From every art in ten townlands and mostly all his lone,
So he'd play the fife for company, and fight King William's wars,
  And study all the queer old days behind King William's throne.
But Billy was no **luny**—he was there when God made brains—
  A bogle couldn't scare him—he heard tell of them before,
And he never thought of fairies only sporting with the weans,
  May-eve at hanging May-flowers for a charm at every door.

But after this thing happened him it give his head a twist;
  Stepping home one night by ghost-light to the tune of *Colleen dhas*,

When he came to Tullygarley brig the Braid was all
    a mist,
    And speech came from the thick of it forbidding
        him to pass.
With a voice that wasn't mortal in a mist—and noth-
    ing more—
    Thinks Billy "There are times to run, and them
        that can't run, prays;
I'm afeard it is a woman," and he either prayed or
    swore,
    "I'm afeard it's not the welcome sort that dresses
        up in stays."

By this the mist was clearing off, and Billy looking
    down
    Sees standing in the flood, or swimming—sorrow
        one knows which—
The loveliest kind of female between that and Lime-
    rick town,
    With the general look and beauty of an Irish water-
        witch.
Says she, "Billy, I am lonesome." "Well," says Billy,
    "I'm afeard
    I haven't seen your family lately," speaking quite
        polite;
"If you like, Mem," he kept talking, picking up and
    feeling cheered
    To see such melting eyes, "I'll post a letter if you'll
        write."

"Och, Billy, that's not it at all. I want to have a
 friend ;
  If you'll come down to the waterside and listen for
   awhile
I'll try and make you sensible how far my powers
  extend,
  And how much we'd help each other," and with
   that she give a smile.
So down went Billy on the bank, just trusting to his
  luck,
  And she led him to a quiet place near where the
   waters meet.
She could swim without a ripple, floating easy as a
  duck,
  But he never found out whether it was with a tail
   or feet.

She kept him and conversed him till the glinting of
  the dawn,
  And trysted him for that night week at Lisnafillan
   Green,
And through that year all round the Maine and Braid
  she led him on,
  With tales of queer outlandish things and words of
   love between.
She must have had a notion of him, seeing all she did,
  And what she told him, how he lived in ages long ago,
A harper to King Brian, and far more his wit kept hid;
  Since people just would laugh, he said, at what
   they didn't know.

He said her name was Moira, and she once had great
  renown,
  And mighty proud she made him with a serpent
    ring of fate,
But what he set most store by was a fife she brought
  him down
  From where it lay below the Boyne since James
    went out of date.
The music Billy made with it was past belief to hear,
  You'd thought the stars were singing when you
    heard him in the dark,
And I've known old David Herbison, the poet, say
  " Ay, dear,
  I'd just as soon hear Billy as a blackbird or a lark."

But Billy's music died away; the silver notes had rest,
  And Dander promised solemnly they'd never sound
    again ;
That he'd take the fife in friendliness, was Billy's last
  request,
  And fling it in the water where the Braid flows in
    the Maine.
And William Dander did it when the moon was sink-
  ing low,
  And a mist swept up the river with a lamentation
    sore ;
The tongue was past man's knowledge, but the mean-
  ing seemed to go—
  " Oh, Billy, you're my darling, but I'll never see you
    more !"

www.ingramcontent.com/pod-product-compliance
Lightning Source LLC
Chambersburg PA
CBHW031442160426
43195CB00010BB/820